THE WORKING MEN'S COLLEGE

AUSPICIUM

MELIORIS

ÆVI.

MDCCCLIV.

Purchased

R.E.Tyler Del. 1913 C.H.Perry Sc.

BATH

1 Bath Abbey from Orange Grove, showing the obelisk "erected in compliment to the Prince of Orange by Mr. Nash": from the plate by J. C. Nattes (1806)

BATH

By

R. A. L. Smith

With 84 Illustrations from
Engravings, Paintings, and Photographs
by Paul Fripp, and others

LONDON
B. T. BATSFORD LTD.
15 NORTH AUDLEY STREET, W.1

TO
JOAN

First published Summer, 1944

MADE AND PRINTED IN GREAT BRITAIN
BY JARROLD AND SONS LTD., NORWICH

Contents

A Note on the Author

THE WRITER OF THIS BOOK, LIEUTENANT R. A. LENDON SMITH, R.N.V.R., died on 28 April, 1944. He was a Fellow of Trinity College, Cambridge, whose last year had been spent in the Naval Intelligence giving lectures at various bases. A mediaevalist of distinction, he had brought out a book on *Canterbury Cathedral Priory, a Study in Monastic Administration*. He was only twenty-eight years of age.

Tony Smith had a great devotion to all English things and an exact and widespread scholarship. His appearance was attractive and very striking, the height, the fair hair slightly thinning, that deep brow and the background of his quiet pallor. A generosity of character founded upon a sympathetic and prevailing gentleness marked his approach and anchored him in his strong untroubled friendships. He had a lucid sincerity and was singularly loyal. Yet with this there went a dynamic quality and one wondered at the scope of his charged enthusiasm.

Working with an intense and channelled energy, he brought to bear upon each subject of his study a sensitive feeling for the English scene, its broad effects, its architectural detail. It was thus that Bath appealed to him. In particular he cherished and understood the high civilized traditions of his country; in this way he was captured by the urbane serene quality of the chosen city.

On a wider plane he had a devotion to and belief in the great citadels of human values; he loved all that passed therein. He had a veneration for England and the Catholic Church, the strong enduring entities of which he was a citizen. Tony Smith was both tranquil and self-spending. His marriage perfected a life which was already rich in friendships with his contemporaries and his seniors. He received and communicated happiness.

DAVID MATHEW

Foreword

I CAN WELL REMEMBER THE FIRST TIME I ENTERED BATH. IT was a very hot day in the summer of 1937 and I was journeying on foot from Glastonbury to Chester. The object of this pilgrimage was to see the great cathedrals, abbeys, and castles of the West Country and the Welsh Marches. Towards the evening of the first day's walk I came to the hills which engirdle the Queen City of the West. Tired and footsore as I was, I lost nothing of that breathtaking moment when the eye first catches sight of the lovely terraced city. Lying, so to speak, in a vast amphitheatre, surrounded by hills of enchanting beauty, it seemed like a city out of an Eastern romance, a new Jerusalem built by some magic hand in England's green and pleasant land. Since then I have visited Bath many times and have gained an intimate familiarity with its streets and squares and crescents. I have come to love it with a deep and genuine love which has made the writing of this book both an unavoidable necessity and an exquisite pleasure.

I wish to express my warmest thanks to Miss P. K. Ellis who has kindly typed the greater part of my manuscript.

R. A. L. S.

14 *October*, 1943.

Acknowledgment

ALL THE PHOTOGRAPHS REPRODUCED IN THIS BOOK ARE THE WORK of Paul Fripp, with the exception of Figs. 7, 35, 83, and 84, which were supplied by Dorien Leigh Ltd.; Figs. 6, 44, 54, by Will F. Taylor; Fig. 30, by F. R. Winstone; Fig. 31, by H. N. King; Fig. 55, by the British Council (photograph by J. Dixon-Scott); Fig. 82, by Time and Life, Ltd. (photograph by Oswald Wild); and Figs. 79, 80, and 81, by the National Buildings Record.

The Publishers must also record their gratitude to the Spa Committee of Bath, for providing prints of the two portraits reproduced on Figs. 15 and 39, and to the Homeland Association Ltd., for the subject on Fig. 27. As in other books, they must express their sincere obligation to Messrs. Walter T. Spencer, of New Oxford Street, for many of the subjects from prints and engravings, reproduced from originals in their unrivalled collection.

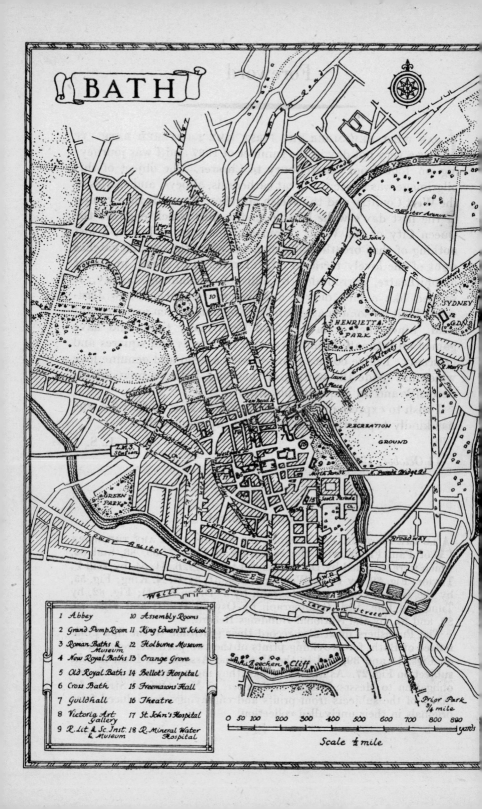

BATH

1 Abbey
2 Grand Pump Room
3 Roman Baths & Museum
4 New Royal Baths
5 Old Royal Baths
6 Cross Bath
7 Guildhall
8 Victoria Art Gallery
9 R. Lit. & Sc. Inst. & Museum
10 Assembly Rooms
11 King Edward VI School
12 Holburne Museum
13 Orange Grove
14 Bellot's Hospital
15 Freemasons' Hall
16 Theatre
17 St. John's Hospital
18 R. Mineral Water Hospital

0 50 100 200 300 400 500 600 700 800 890 yards

Scale ½ mile

Bath Panorama

THERE IS NO MORE BEAUTIFUL SIGHT IN ENGLAND THAN the whole panorama of Bath viewed from the lofty summit of Beechen Cliff. If, like Catherine Morland and Eleanor and Henry Tilney in Jane Austen's *Persuasion*, we ascend "that noble hill, whose beautiful verdure and hanging coppice render it so striking an object from almost every opening in Bath", few of us could exercise such self-denial as the impressionable Catherine, who, after a lecture on perspective from Henry, "voluntarily rejected the whole city of Bath as unworthy to make part of a landscape".

Here, on the top of Beechen Cliff, it is like being on the Mount of Olives, with the sacred city lying at our feet. The classic beauty of the Queen City of the West displays itself in all its noble splendour. The winding Avon, threading its way along the valley like a silvery coil; the venerable Abbey, grey and massive and impregnable, "The Lantern of England"; terrace after terrace rising in perfect symmetry from the valley to the hills. There is something here of the glory of Greece and Rome: of the dignity and nobility and austerity of the classic past from which our civilization has sprung.

Bath has known every age in our island story. The Roman set foot here and created *Aquae Sulis* for those in search of health and pleasure. The Saxon conqueror succeeded him, at first with dark and malevolent design: then he too became a humble suppliant at the healing springs. Monks and bishops followed in his wake. Bath became an ecclesiastical centre of the medieval world: an episcopal see with a monastic chapter. The centuries rolled by and, strange metamorphosis, Bath became the metropolis of fashion and folly; the rendezvous of Polite Society; the scene of the life and death of the immortal Beau Nash. Then fashion was ousted by respectability and Bath became a city fit for Jane Austen's heroines to live in. The great wastes of the Victorian age lay ahead, and Bath

subsided into a provincial city, remarkable more for her loveliness and her charms than her Polite Society. She remains
to-day in her architecture, her history, and her tradition, a
perfect epitome of our national past: an harbinger of an even
greater future.

2   Bath Stone and Bath Chair: The Royal Crescent

3   Bath Abbey, seen over the Rooftops

1

Roman Bath

BATH MUST HAVE BEEN FAMED FOR ITS HOT MINERAL SPRINGS long before the conquering Roman legions set foot upon the shores of Britain. The neighbourhood abounds in camps and earthworks of remote Celtic origin. Sul, the tutelary goddess of the springs, was created by the rich imagination of the Somerset folk many years before the Roman occupation. She is found nowhere else in the vast confines of the Roman Empire. But, beyond the fact of the existence of her cult, nothing is known of Bath in the time of the ancient Britons.

Happily legend has been able to improve on history, for Bath, like Rome and London, has a foundation myth that has profoundly gripped the imagination of its citizens. The mythical founder of Bath, the lovely city that lies nearly tucked in the fold of the River Avon, was no less a personage than Bladud the son of Lud Hudibras, King of Britain, and the great-grandson of Aeneas. A prince of great virtue and distinguished appearance, Bladud was beloved of the courtiers and the devoted heir-apparent of his father. By some unhappy chance he contracted the loathsome disease of leprosy and was thus obliged to leave his father's court, lest all there should become infected by the malady. His mother, the Queen, who had not despaired of his recovery, attached a brilliant ring to his finger before he left so that he might make himself known on his return. After many wanderings Bladud arrived at Keynsham, a village about six miles from Bath, and offered his services as a swineherd to one of the inhabitants. Soon, alas!, he discovered that he had imparted his leprosy to the herd and, dreading the anger of his patron, drove the pigs to the opposite side of the river on the pretext that the acorns were finer there. And so Bladud and his herd came to the massive and thickly-wooded hills which hung over the northern side of Bath. The swine, which were quick to discern the health-giving springs, plunged into the muddy

11

morass and were only induced to return to their master by the sight of a bag of acorns. Having washed the mud off the swine, Bladud discovered to his astonished surprise that they were now rid of the leprosy. Hastily profiting from their example and bathing in the muddy swamp, he had the indescribable pleasure of finding that his leprosy was cured in like manner. So Bladud returned to his father's court and was received with rapture by all. He then proceeded to Bath, cleaned the springs, erected baths, and laid the foundations of a noble and elegant city.

Besides his adventure with the pigs which ended in the foundation of Bath, Bladud has another claim on our gratitude. He deserves no less a title than *The Father of Aviation*. Let Geoffrey of Monmouth tell the tale:

"He was for ever devising some new wonder, and by and by he gave out that he was about to fly in the air like a bird. So he had wings made to his own destruction. He fitted on his pinions and mounted in the air with a strong and bold flight. But lo! he fell in with contrary winds, and his strength failed; the strings snapped, his rigging got out of order, and down he fell. He pitched on the roof of Apollo's temple, and was dashed to pieces."

The glorious life and spectacular death of Bladud made a deep impression on the Woods, the chief creators of the architectural magnificence of eighteenth-century Bath, and one of their greatest achievements, the Circus, is crowned by a series of stone acorns. It is indeed true to say that belief in Bladud formed part of the creed of every true Bath man. There is a manuscript in the British Museum of the Bladud legend which contains the following note:

"We whose names are hereunder written, natives of the city of Bath, having perused the above tradition, do think it very truly and faithfully related—as witness our hands this first day of November 1741."

Thus did credulity and civic pride strangely coalesce.

The evidence that can be gained from coins and inscriptions shows clearly that Bath was occupied by the Romans at an early stage of the conquest. The arresting name of *Aquae Sulis*— the Waters of Sul—was given by the Romans to the place whence issued the hot and life-giving springs. Probably Romano-

British life existed here as early as the reigns of Claudius (A.D. 41–54) and Nero (A.D. 54–68) and reached something of a climax at the end of the century when the statesmanlike Agricola, commander of the province of Britain in the years 78–84, carried out a deliberate and calculated policy of Romanization. The Roman historian Tacitus reveals the subtle technique of Agricola in enervating and undermining the morale of the conquered Britons.

"In order that a race of rude and primitive men, versed in the arts of war, might be rendered peaceful and tranquil through the delights of luxury, he privately encouraged and officially helped them to build temples, market-places, and houses, praising the eager and admonishing the slothful. And so imitation became a matter of compulsion. For now, indeed, he instructed the sons of chieftains in the liberal arts and confronted British native wit with Gallic learning, so that only those who were unfamiliar with the Roman tongue were regarded as lacking in eloquence. Then they were made to adopt our style of dressing and the toga became common. Little by little they were lured to the blandishments of vice, to porticoes and baths, and to luxurious feasts. In this way an unsophisticated people learnt to mistake the path of servitude for the highroad to culture."

It is easy to see how Aquae Sulis fits into this picture. Everything goes to show that it was the place specially chosen by the Romans for the enervation of the Britons as well as for the needful relaxation of the legionaries.

We must try to see Roman Britain in something like a true perspective. Britain was a remote and relatively unimportant province of the Roman Empire, chiefly valuable for its granaries and its supplies of lead from the Mendip Hills and of tin from the Cornish mines. It was a land of small country towns and of large country estates and all the settled civilized life lay in the south-east and south-west. Wales and the north of Britain were inhabited only by the unlettered native population and the Roman legionaries, who at their full complement were 40,000 strong. Aquae Sulis belonged, of course, to the settled civilized southern part of England. It was easy of access, as the great Roman road the Fosse was so constructed as to run obliquely from the north-east to the south-west of the country, joining the four towns of Lincoln, Leicester, Bath, and Exeter. Bath was indeed easier to reach in Roman times than at any time before the end of the eighteenth century.

Pious local antiquarians, glorying in the fair name of Aquae Sulis, have sought to make of it a second Rome, endowing it with all manner of wonderful buildings. The truth is simpler and far less romantic. Aquae Sulis, far from being a second Rome or even a second London or Colchester, was a small town of something less than 23 acres. No legionaries were ever quartered here and there was no *prætorium*. Nor was there, as many local writers love to claim, a flourishing *fabrica armorum* or armament factory. The existence of a *forum* on the site of the present Abbey Churchyard and of a *basilica* on the site of the present Abbey Church is, in the words of an eminent modern archaeologist, "neither provable nor probable". All these are mere conjectures and vain imaginings, having no shred of evidence to support them.

It is, however, certain that Aquae Sulis was a walled town. In 1795 part of the Roman north wall was discovered below the foundations of the medieval wall opposite the Royal Mineral Water Hospital. Later, another part of the Roman north wall came to light. It is perhaps a fair guess that the Roman and medieval walls were roughly coincident, enclosing a pentagonal area bounded on two sides by the silvery waters of the River Avon. In spite of its straight lines, so reminiscent of Roman work, the main street-plan of modern Bath in no way reproduces that of Aquae Sulis. Stall Street actually lies on top of the Roman baths and Union Street is of very recent origin.

A number of private houses have been excavated, mostly in the region of the Mineral Water Hospital. There are some good mosaics and an abundance of Samian earthenware. All the evidence points to Aquae Sulis as a town consisting of a small group of houses inhabited by the officials of the baths and temple, by a few residents, and by visitors who had come to take the waters. There was no independent municipal life. Everything led up to and centred in the baths and the temple of their tutelary goddess Sul-Minerva.

The Bath waters, which are reputed to be wonderfully rich in radio-active material, gush hot and bubbling to the surface

4, 5 Corston: a typical Village of the Mendip Country, near Bath

6   The Roman Bath

from a very great depth. No one can say how great that depth is, but it is thought that they proceed directly from the volcanic strata of the earth. The waters are said to be suitable for drinking and bathing and few will dispute that they are excellent for bathing. Many, however, have found from sad experience that they are far from pleasant to drink. Others—not only local patriots—will be heard to praise the waters to the skies. Some even—the writer recalls a case in point—will venture to contrast them favourably with the red wines of Burgundy! Whatever may be the tastes of to-day, and they vary from warm enthusiasm to cordial dislike, there can be no question that the Romans, for reasons that have already been given, developed Aquae Sulis as a spa and a watering-place in much the same way, for example, as they created Aquae Bormonis in central Gaul.

The waters, which pour forth at the rate of half-a-million gallons a day, arose in Roman times from a spring which is now in the centre of the King's Bath. An excellent view of this spring, with a statue of the inevitable Bladud looming in the background, can be obtained from the south window of the present Pump Room. A flight of stairs to the east of the building leads to the remains of the Roman baths. Something of an anti-climax must be expected. When the eyes first become accustomed to the gloom of the dungeon-like apartment that serves as a sub-vault to the Pump Room, it is only to make the horrifying discovery that such priceless archaeological treasures as the famous Bath Gorgon are dumped here, ill-guarded and ill-preserved. Then, when one has had time to explore further, the view is rudely arrested by the sight of the thoroughly flat and depressing sculptured figures of the Roman emperors with which modern ill-taste has sought to embellish the Roman baths. But the worst is now over. A detailed examination of the Roman bathing-establishment, which despite the lapse of nearly two thousand years has been rendered wonderfully complete by the skill of recent excavators, will most amply repay any pain that may have been caused by its unfortunate setting. Little wonder that Solinus, a Roman writer of the third century, included Bath and its waters among the wonders of the world! No more remarkable relic of Roman civilization exists in Britain and it would be fairly hard to rival anywhere on the Continent. The general impression is one of tremendous material achievement, of technical ability of the very highest order. And withal a power, a dignity, a majesty, that all too rarely accompany great engineering skill.

The principal or *Great Bath* is situated in the very centre of the bathing establishment. This the Romans must have used for swimming and immersion. A stone platform, with steps leading to the water, makes a most effective diving-board. The floor is still covered with the lead placed there by the Romans, and you can even see part of the lead pipe which conducted the water from the spring to the bath. It is easy to marvel over the finely-articulated hollow bricks that formed the arches and which have survived in such abundance. Ruined as it is, the Great Bath retains a great deal of its former elegance and a singular sense of dignity and proportion.

To the west of the Great Bath lies the attractive *Circular Bath*, much smaller in size and less ambitious in design. Several other baths and chambers are also situated in these parts. At the east end of the building are the hypocausts and *sudatoria* or sweating-chambers: wonders of exact craftsmanship and technical skill. It is not difficult to picture Tacitus' Britons undergoing their course of enervation in such luxurious surroundings. How fatally easy it would be to succumb to these delightful pleasures!

It would be fascinating to know whether the Roman baths were built by private capitalists or by public subscription and enterprise. Unfortunately there is simply no evidence to guide us. As municipal life was practically non-existent at Aquae Sulis, one may perhaps suppose that some adventurous capitalist, conscious of the commercial and publicity value of the hot springs, "cashed in" on Agricola's Romanizing campaign and made a going concern of the baths. How was the bathing at Aquae Sulis conducted? Was there mixed bathing or were the two sexes severely segregated? The analogy of other watering-places in the Empire would seem to suggest that the Romans, like the Watch Committees of many a modern seaside resort, frowned on the practice of mixed bathing and allotted different hours for male and female. Difficult as it first may seem to picture Roman matrons in the rôle of Mrs. Grundy, who would be rash enough to deny that Aquae Sulis, the adopted city of Beau Nash, was once the centre of a vigorous purity campaign led by these austere ladies?

When it is asked who visited the baths, numerous inscriptions are at hand to supply the answer. Many of the visitors were Roman legionaries who sought refuge from the rigours and cold blasts of the north in the sheltered valley of the Avon. Thus we know of three soldiers who came from the Sixth Legion at York and three who came from the Twentieth Legion at Chester. Long vigils on the Wall and in northern camps would have made men used to the warm sunny climes of Mediterranean lands an easy prey to rheumatism and other complaints. Little wonder, then, that they sought the hot springs of Aquae Sulis as a sovereign remedy! Other visitors of whom notice remains are a town-councillor from Gloucester and a sculptor from Cirencester—professional men seeking a brief vacation and health-cure. Some even came from abroad, from Trier, Metz, Chartres, and all the regions of northern Gaul. Nothing bears more convincing witness to the fame and importance of Aquae Sulis in Roman times than the wide diversity of its *clientèle*. Men of every occupation and class flocked here from afar. And to this continual flow of visitors must be added the small group of old gentlemen, sufferers from chronic gout or rheumatism, who resided permanently at Aquae Sulis in the fervent hope that the waters would one day effect a permanent cure. These aged valetudinarians are to be found in every age and every season, in the Bath of Beau Nash and Jane Austen as well as in the Bath of Agricola.

It was not only the baths that drew men from great distances to Aquae Sulis. The temple of Sul, the patroness of the springs, was one of the most famous shrines in Britain, a centre of prayer and pilgrimage. Perhaps even before the Roman occupation the cult of Sul was associated with immersion in the waters. Certain it is that the Romans identified Sul with Minerva, the goddess of healing, just as they identified the Celtic warrior-gods with Mars. The great importance which the Romans attached to the cult of Sul-Minerva is shown by the fact that only her temple and the official temple of Claudius at Colchester were built on the grand classical model. The shrines of all the other Romano-British deities were much smaller and simpler in design. It is also rather surprising to discover that the fires of Sul-Minerva's temple were stoked not with wood, but with coal. Here Solinus is our authority. He says: "In Britain are hot springs furnished luxuriously for human use. Over these springs Minerva presides, and in her temple the perpetual fire never whitens into ash, but as the flame fades, turns into rocky balls." Now beyond question the "rocky balls" are the cinders of the local Somersetshire coal.

The temple of Sul-Minerva, of which enough remains for a fairly complete reconstruction to be made, was built in the Corinthian style with a façade of four columns, fluted pilasters, and a richly designed frieze. A remarkable pediment or gable-end of the temple has survived. This consists of a shield which appears to have been supported on either side by a winged figure like a Victory. Beneath the shield is a space filled by a helmet on the left side and on the right by a small owl—the bird of Minerva. In the centre is the *pièce de résistance*. A huge gorgon head, ferocious and barbaric, with head and beard intertwined with snakes, proclaims another of the attributes of Minerva. This is the famous Bath Gorgon. It is unquestionably the *chef d'œuvre* of Romano-British sculpture. In its fierce intensity, its rich imaginative power, the Bath Gorgon departs completely from the accepted conventions of the classical tradition. The gorgon-head of conventional art is always female, while this is the male head of an untamed barbarian. Even in its present sorry situation—hidden away in the dark basement— the fierce staring eyes arrest the attention of the most cursory onlooker. What must it not have been like "when it stood aloft blazing with colour like a Celtic enamel"?

Several of the altars erected by pious worshippers of Sul-Minerva are still extant. One of these commemorates the *Sulevae* or spirits of Sul, who were said to preside over the rivers, hills, and villages in the neighbourhood of Aquae Sulis. There is a funeral-stone of one Calpurnius Receptus, a priest of the goddess Sul. This seems to indicate that her cult was organized with a hierarchy of attendant priests. A charming sideline on the worship of Sul is afforded by the votive altars which two freedmen erected for their master Aufidius Maximus in thanksgiving for their manumission. Other deities were worshipped at Aquae Sulis—Mars, Hercules, and the Divine Emperor,—but Sul-Minerva and her temple reigned supreme, easily eclipsing other gods and their votaries.

The last days of Roman Bath are lost in impenetrable obscurity. Coins show that the site was occupied until at least the year 400. Then darkness descends. We cannot even tell whether Aquae Sulis was abandoned like Silchester at the sight of the invading Angles and Saxons or whether it was the scene of a hideous massacre. An English poem of the eighth century, which is of little value as evidence, suggests the latter grim alternative "Death destroyeth all". Certain it is that the English invaders conquered the neighbourhood of Bath about the year 577. The place cannot have been inhabited by de-Romanized Britons after that date and was probably deserted long before.

What, then, was the fate of the Roman baths? They gradually silted up, the roofs and walls collapsed, and a dense undergrowth covered the *débris*. Wild fowl nested in the ruins and these splendid and luxurious buildings became the abode of the coot and the teal. All memory of the baths was completely obliterated. Aquae Sulis, like an insubstantial pageant, faded and left not a rack behind.

2

Medieval Bath

THE DARKNESS WHICH DESCENDS UPON BATH AFTER THE departure of the Romans is for long unrelieved by historical record. Not a glimmer of light peers through the blackness of the night. Then suddenly a swift searchlight is thrown upon the old Roman city of Aquae Sulis by the compiler of the *Anglo-Saxon Chronicle*, who records of the year 577 that

"This year Cuthwine and Ceawlin fought with the Britons, and slew three kings, Coinmail, and Condidan, and Farinmail, on the spot that is called Deorham, and took from them three cities, Gloucester, Cirencester, and Bath."

The reference is typical of the confused and turbulent period of the Anglo-Saxon conquest. It was an age of confused skirmishes and counter-invasions. Anarchy was master of the scene and law and order were never more in abeyance.

During the Anglo-Saxon centuries Bath re-emerges under the names of *Akemanceaster* or *Hatum Bathum*, from which the modern name is derived. It acquired some fame both as a civic and ecclesiastical centre for the West of England. At least as early as the beginning of the tenth century the city was presided over by a reeve or *gerefa*, an official of no mean importance in the Saxon hierarchy. There was a *tun-moot*, where the common affairs of the city were discussed and decided, and a mint for the coining of money. One has the impression of a small country town with local interests in retail trade.

The date when Christianity was introduced into Bath cannot be determined with any accuracy. It is safe to assume that this cannot have occurred much before the middle of the seventh century, when the West Country was first systematically evangelized by the missionaries who followed in the wake of St. Augustine. In the following century we hear of a church at Bath served by secular priests. This probably occupied the site of the present Abbey Church. It was perhaps in the early part of the tenth century that the Black Monks of St. Benedict came to occupy and serve this church. Their appearance in Bath, whenever it may have occurred, marks the beginning of a new era. For six centuries and more the old Roman watering-place, which was later to become the metropolis of fashion under the magic hand of Beau Nash, was first and foremost a monastic borough, living in the shade of a great Benedictine monastery. Here in 944 came a band of monks from the great abbey of St. Bertin of Ghent, fleeing from the austerities imposed upon them by St. Gerard of Brogne. The influence of these Flemish monks made such a deep impression at Bath that even at the time of the Norman conquest the Flemish style of writing was still in vogue at the abbey.

The great event in the pre-Conquest history of Bath was the crowning of King Edgar in the Abbey Church in 973. The two archbishops Dunstan and Oswald officiated at the ceremony in the presence of a vast crowd of priests, monks, nobles, and layfolk. The chronicler blossomed into verse for the occasion:

"Here was Edgar, of Angles lord,
With courtly pomp hallow'd to king
At Akemanceaster, the ancient city;
Whose modern sons, dwelling therein,
Have named her BATH.
Much bliss was there by all enjoyed
On that happy day named Pentecost
By men below.
A crowd of priests, a throng of monks,
I understand, in counsel sage were gather'd there."

The feasting and the junketing at this splendid ceremony were lovingly recalled by many generations of Bathonians. When Leland visited Bath in the early sixteenth century he discovered that the citizens prayed in all their official rites for the soul of King Edgar. "And", he tells us, "at Whitsunday-tyde, at the which tyme men say that Edgar there was crounid, ther is a King electid at Bath every yere of the Tounes men in the joyfulle remembraunce of King Edgar and the Privileges gyven to the Toun by hym. This King is festid and his Adherentes by the richest Menne of the Toun". A charming instance of our ancestors' ingenuity in finding a good excuse for a carousal!

At the end of the tenth century a singularly lovable man
became abbot of Bath. His name was Aelfheah, who is better
known to Englishmen of to-day as St. Elphege, the saintly
archbishop of Canterbury who won the crown of martyrdom
when the fierce Danish warriors besieged and captured his
cathedral city in 1011. It was some thirty years earlier, about
980, that Elphege became abbot of Bath. He had been a monk
at Deerhurst but had rebelled against the lax way of life at that
house. He resolved to save his soul and to perfect his spirit in
solitary contemplation of God; but, as so often happened with
the chosen spirits of the Middle Ages, disciples gathered around
him and he was finally prevailed upon to become the abbot of
Bath. His reign there lasted for some four years before he went
by way of Winchester to his martyr's death at Canterbury.
His saintly gentle spirit must have made a deep and abiding
impression upon the monastic community. Never again was
such heroic sanctity to flourish at Bath.

Just before the Norman conquest the town of Bath was in the
hands of Edith, the queen of Edward the Confessor and the
daughter of the powerful Earl Godwin. When, however, Edward
fell out with Godwin and banished him from the kingdom, he saw
fit to shut up his queen in a nunnery and to confiscate her dower.
So when Domesday was compiled in 1086 Bath was a royal
borough. We are told that

"The King holds Bath. In the time of King Edward it was
taxed at the rate of twenty hides, when the county of Somerset
was assessed. Here the king has twenty-four burgesses, paying
him four pounds by the year, and there are ninety burgesses under
the protection of other men, paying there sixty shillings per annum.
The king has there six unoccupied houses."

The record shows plainly that Bath had suffered like many
other English towns in the general disorder and devastation that
followed the Conquest. Its woes were only aggravated in 1088
when Robert of Mowbray and his followers, who had rebelled
against the arbitrary rule of William Rufus, plundered the city
and laid waste the neighbouring countryside with fire and sword.
At this period Bath must have sunk to its lowest ebb since the
last days of the Roman occupation. Abandoned houses, deserted
streets: on all sides the visible evidence of fire and destruction.

Who could recognize that gay and joyous city in which King
Edgar the Peaceful had been crowned with such pomp and
splendour?

Yet at this dark hour a saviour was at hand in the person of a
Frenchman, John of Tours. It came about in this wise. John,
a native of Tours who was highly skilled in the practice of
medicine, served William Rufus well for a number of years in
the capacity of a chaplain. In return for his services the Red
King promoted John in 1088 to the episcopal see of Somerset,
which for some two centuries had been located at Wells and had
just fallen vacant through the death of the Lotharingian prelate
Gisa. Now some thirteen years previously the bishops of the
English province, meeting in council at London, had decided
upon the policy of moving episcopal sees from villages and small
towns into large and important cities. Although three sees were
immediately removed from country to city in 1075 no further
progress was made for a number of years owing to the absence
of the King in his duchy of Normandy and to other factors
which stood in the way of ecclesiastical changes. In 1088,
however, all was ripe for further changes and John of Tours,
newly consecrated to the bishopric and enjoying the personal
confidence of the King, was unwilling to rule his diocese from
the small town of Wells, so remote from the main stream of ecclesiastical and secular activities in the west of England. He
therefore secured from William Rufus the grant of Bath Abbey,
vacant through the death of the abbot Alfsige, and transferred
his see from Wells to Bath, setting up his episcopal throne in the
Abbey Church. A year or so later John purchased the whole city
of Bath, with its customs, tolls, and mint, from the King for a
sum of £60 and so consolidated his position in the cathedral city.

It is difficult to form a consistent impression of the character
of John of Tours. William of Malmesbury testifies to his generosity, his learning, and his general good nature while admitting,
with other contemporary authorities, his quite exceptional blind-
ness and insensitiveness to the feelings of others. His behaviour
towards the canons of Wells was truly shocking. Not content
with depriving them of the bulk of their revenues, he ruthlessly
destroyed their houses, tore down their refectory, dormitory,
cellarium, cloisters, and other buildings in order to build himself

a palace, and compelled them to make shift for themselves as best they might in the houses of the citizens. One authority, indeed, tells us that John subsequently repented of these arbitrary actions, but there is no evidence that he performed any act of restitution to the outraged canons. On the contrary, we know that his relations were quartered on the lands of the canons for some time after his death. At Bath his attitude to the monks was at first one of hostility. He dubbed them dolts and barbarians, confiscated much of their land, and even deprived them of their customary allowances of food. Gradually, however, he came to have a juster appreciation of the monastic life. In 1106 he restored all the property which he had snatched from the monks and even endowed the cathedral priory with new lands. He was also at pains to encourage learning in the monastery, "rejoicing", as William of Malmesbury says, "in the society of learned men". His community acquired an enviable reputation for learning and scholarship. It also throve in material prosperity, for when John of Tours was bishop and titular abbot of the monastery benefactions were showered upon it, ranging from small gifts of land to the grant of Dunster Priory by William of Mohun and his wife Adeliza in 1090.

The architectural achievements of John of Tours matched his zeal for learning. During his long episcopate, which lasted from 1088 to 1122, the monastic church of Bath, which had probably suffered badly in the general devastation wrought by Robert of Mowbray's band, was entirely rebuilt on a greatly enlarged plan with an ample precinct. Its size and magnificence were in every way appropriate to a cathedral priory of the first rank. The length of its nave was only surpassed by that of the great monastic cathedral churches of Winchester, Ely, and Norwich. The present church at Bath, which was built during the sixteenth century, only covers the nave-space of John of Tours' structure, part of which can still be seen embedded in the masonry at the end of the south aisle of the choir. A grandness of design and proportion characterized the whole building and John of Tours generously applied the revenues of his episcopal table to the fabric fund of his new cathedral church. Thus at Bath Bishop John, once he had conquered his initial prejudice against the monastic community, showed himself a true benefactor and an enlightened ruler. His genius for organization came at a providential moment and he proved himself equal to the task of transforming Bath from a largely derelict town into an important and prosperous cathedral city.

The work of John of Tours fixed the essential character of Bath for over four centuries as a monastic and episcopal city. The grey walls of the abbey, rising massively in the very centre of the town, bear most eloquent witness to the timelessness and indefectibility of the Church of Christ. Amidst all the changes of fortune and fashion to which Bath has been subject, there they have remained: the one element of continuity in the flux of time. Close to the walls of the monastery on the south-west side there stood the bishop's palace. This also had been built by John of Tours but fell into decay when from the thirteenth century onwards the bishops normally dwelt at Wells. In Leland's time (c. 1540) only "one gret square Tour of it with other Ruines yet appere".

In the twelfth and thirteenth centuries there was a ding-dong battle between the monks of Bath and the canons of Wells on electoral rights and questions of precedence and title. Both claimed that the bishop should have his see and be enthroned in their church, from which alone he should take his title. The dispute was lively and sustained: tempers were frayed and finally lost on both sides. At this point Pope Adrian IV intervened and at some time before 1159 decreed that

(a) The two churches of Bath and Wells should be equally seats of the bishop.

(b) The bishop was to be elected by representatives of the two chapters.

(c) The prior of Bath was to notify the election to the archbishop of Canterbury.

(d) The bishop was to be enthroned in both churches, and first in the church of Bath.

This compromise, so admirably suited to the temper of Englishmen, seemed to satisfy both parties. When, however, the monks of Bath tried to steal a march on the canons of Wells in 1192 by electing a bishop of their own accord, a furore arose and pandemonium reigned for some time. A final settlement did not occur until 1245 when another Pope, Innocent IV, decreed that the ruling of his predecessor should stand and that the full title of Bath and Wells should in future be inscribed on the seal of the bishop. Hence the present title of the see. During this period a similar dispute ranged between the monks of Coventry and the canons of Lichfield on the same questions. Our medieval ancestors were rarely prepared to concede a point, though ever ready to catch others napping!

The bishop of Bath and Wells was titular abbot of the monastic community at Bath. But from the end of the twelfth century onwards he rarely resided at Bath, so the prior of Bath was normally the *de facto* abbot of the monastery. The bishop kept the right of appointing the prior in his own hands until 1261, when he gave this privilege to the monks. He always retained the right of appointing the sacrist and the precentor, two of the most important monastic officials. The bishop was therefore more than a merely nominal head of Bath cathedral priory (the term Bath Abbey is strictly a misnomer for a house where there was no direct abbatial government), though the constant daily control of the affairs of the house was left to his subordinate, the prior.

The *raison d'être* of a great Benedictine cathedral priory like Bath was the recitation of the Divine Office in choir by the whole of the community of monks. The ceaseless praise of God and the constant daily toil represented the lofty ideal which St. Benedict had set before his sons. If at Bath, as elsewhere, this ideal was sometimes more honoured in the breach than the observance, no discerning student of the Middle Ages can fail to observe how greatly the squalor and cruelty of medieval life were softened and sweetened by the offices of religion. At no period in human history has a higher ideal been set before men. And men must be judged by their ideals as well as by their shortcomings. In this respect we of to-day can learn much from our medieval forebears.

The number of monks at Bath Priory varied from age to age. At the beginning of the thirteenth century there were 41 monks, but this number gradually dwindled and the Black Death of 1349 had a devastating effect at Bath as in so many other places. It reduced the numbers of monks by about a half, and although there was a slight rally, the house never attained its previous size. The priory contained 17 brethren in 1377, 26 in 1447, 21 in 1499, 22 in 1525, and 21 at the time of the Dissolution in 1539. The average for the later Middle Ages was therefore about 25 monks: a house of fair size, but small compared with such great Benedictine abbeys as Glastonbury, St. Albans, and Bury St. Edmunds.

From the secular standpoint the prior of Bath was in the way of being a feudal baron. He had his own separate house and his own counsellors and retinue of servants. He mixed freely with the great ones of the neighbourhood and was, so to say, a figure of consequence in West Country society. His frequent journeyings on behalf of the priory must have made him very well known to all who dwelt in the Bath area. A close supervision of the priory estates, all of which lay in the shires of Somerset and Gloucester, and a keen regard for market prices and possibilities, were both essential duties for the priors of Bath. All could not be expected to rise to the occasion and the ups and downs of the financial history of Bath Priory are partly to be explained by the varying characters of its priors. Great sanctity and great business efficiency are seldom found together. The history of Bath Priory sometimes, alas!, shows clear evidence of the absence of both.

All the great monastic houses were divided into a number of different departments with separate revenues, each of which was placed in charge of a special monastic official. These monk-officers were known as obedientiaries, by reason of their vow of formal obedience to the head of their house. When Bath Priory was at the height of its influence and size in the twelfth and thirteenth centuries it had many obedientiaries. For example, in 1206, besides the prior and a sub-prior and third prior who assisted him in his work of general supervision, there was a treasurer who looked after the finances; a chamberlain and a cellarer who attended to the clothing and feeding of the monks; an infirmarian who looked after those who were sick; a precentor and a sacrist who cared for the church and its services; a garnerer who saw to the receipt of the corn supplies; a refectorarian who had charge of the refectory; a warden of the works who supervised the upkeep of the fabric of the church and monastery;

and an almoner who disbursed alms on behalf of the monks to the poor at the priory-gate. Each obedientiary was in theory independent in his own department, accountable only to the treasurers and to the monastic chapter. In practice, however, there was a great deal of overlapping of departments and often a considerable confusion of finances. In the fifteenth century, when the number of monks had dwindled to about half their former size, several departments were amalgamated and put under the charge of the same officer. Just before the Dissolution, as we shall see later, a gallant attempt was made by Bishop Oliver King to rationalize the whole expenditure of the priory.

Most of the alms given by the monks to the poor probably consisted of food and clothing and not lump sums of money. On at least nineteen days in the year the monks of Bath fed a hundred poor persons in commemoration of the great benefactors of their house. And there was always the splendid and symbolic ceremony of Maundy Thursday when the monks washed the feet of the poor who gathered in the church. Much of their practical charity to the outside world went in the maintenance of the Hospital of St. John the Baptist, which had been founded by Bishop Reginald at the end of the twelfth century to accommodate those poor persons who came to Bath for its healing waters. The extent of monastic almsgiving has been wildly exaggerated by writers on medieval monasticism of the "Mass and Maypole" school, but it is wise not to incline to the other extreme and to ignore the deeds of charity that actually were performed.

It was a common practice in medieval England for the King to appoint certain old retainers as life-pensioners in the larger monasteries of the land. These compulsory guests were known as corrodians because they enjoyed a corrody: what we should to-day refer to as "bed and board". In 1302 Edward I nominated one of his old servants, John of Windsor, who appeared to be at death's door, to a corrody at Bath Priory. The sequel has its amusing side, for, in the words of the editor of the cartulary of the priory, "The Bath waters must have agreed wonderfully with him, for he seems to have lived at the priory for about 34 years, and all that time was kept at the expense of the convent". The next corrodian, John le Harpour, lived for 23 years within the priory walls. No wonder the monks saw fit to engage the King in a lawsuit, denying his right to impose such intolerable burdens!

The relations of the monks of Bath with the city authorities were not, it is to be feared, always amicable. Besides intermittent disputes over property rights, a fierce quarrel broke out in 1408 over the ringing of bells. The prior claimed that the priory had the right of tolling their bells first and last in the city: none of the parish churches were to ring theirs until they had received the signal from the monastic church. The mayor and citizens planned to undermine this scheme by ringing their bells at all hours before and after those of the priory. The struggle raged for many years and was not finally settled until 1421, when a royal inquisition upheld the claims of the prior. Something of the rude vigour of medieval life is revealed to us by the extreme acrimony with which these petty disputes were conducted.

Both the priory and the city of Bath were actively concerned in the trade in wool and cloth which flourished in the West Country in the later Middle Ages. There is plenty of evidence that the monks of Bath dealt in wool on a considerable scale. In 1334, for example, we find the prior buying 300 sacks of wool from a dealer in Malmesbury and three years later he bought 600 sacks from the same person. A number of bonds pledging the priory to the payment of so many sacks of wool at a certain date have survived among the monastic records. Monk's Mill, which stood to the east of the cathedral church on the banks of the Avon until the eighteenth century, was a fulling-mill which in the medieval period lay under the complete control of the monks.

The fame of Bath as a centre of the West of England cloth trade has been immortalized by Geoffrey Chaucer in the Tale of the Wife of Bath in his celebrated *Canterbury Tales*. Her appearance and characteristic outlook are familiar to generations of English folk who have imbibed their Chaucer along with Shakespeare and the Bible. They will gladly recall that

> "Of clooth-making she hadde swiche an haunt,
> She passed hem of Ypres and of Gaunt."

and that

> "Bold was hir face, and fair, and reed of hewe.
> She was a worthy woman at hir lyve
> Housbondes at chirche-dore she hadde fyve."

A woman with such a matrimonial record was hardly likely to sing the praises of virginity and in fact her long and rambling prologue is nothing less than a frontal attack on that state of perfection. She reminds her fellow-pilgrims of "that gentil text" *increase and multiply*, commends the wisdom and example of Solomon, and echoes the Apostle's sentiment that it is better to marry than to burn. This inspires her to describe in great detail her relations with each one of her five husbands. The fifth clearly, gave her most satisfaction, for

> ". . . in our bed he was so fresh and gay"

She was, however, ready for more.

> "Welcome the sixte, whan that ever he shal.
> For sothe, I wol nat kepe me chast in al; .
> Whan myn housbond is fro the world y-gon
> Som Cristen man shal wedde me anon."

Here you have, in the ample person of the Wife of Bath, a passion for marriage that must be truly shocking to our modern sex reformers!

It remains to say something on the medieval city of Bath, in so far as the somewhat meagre records can assist us. The city, it will be remembered, had been purchased from the King by Bishop John of Tours in about the year 1090. It had been surrendered to the Crown by Bishop Savaric in 1192, but almost a hundred years later it reverted to the bishop, who held it until the time of the Reformation. Its municipal development was closely paralleled by that of other English towns. At least as early as 1220 there was a Mayor and Corporation at Bath and the city enjoyed extensive privileges from the grant of King and bishop. No one will be prepared to accept the description of the city given to a French youth about to tour England at the end of the twelfth century.

> "Bath, situated, or rather buried, in deep valleys in the middle of a thick atmosphere and a sulphureous fog, is at the gates of Hell."

Life there may have been uncomfortable and primitive: it was not, in the literal sense, hellish!

Besides the cathedral church there appear to have been five parish churches in medieval Bath: St. Mary de Stalls (now demolished), the official church of the Mayor and Coporation at the corner of Cheap Street and Stall Street; St. Mary at North-gate, St. Michael within, and St. Michael without, the Walls; and the church of St. James. These parish churches have either been destroyed or modernized beyond recognition. They display no evidence of their medieval past. But this is not the case with the Magdalen chapel on the long hill called Holloway at the south side of the city well outside the walls. This windswept little building, which contains some very graceful perpendicular work, was used by the priors of Bath as a private chapel in the later Middle Ages. It had previously been a house for lepers: thus its remote situation. It is one of those little gems that the casual visitor to Bath is so apt to miss.

If we wish to gain an idea of Bath at the very end of the medieval period as it appeared to a discerning and practised traveller, we cannot do better than follow John Leland in his tour of the city during the reign of Henry VIII. This inde-fatigable antiquary entered Bath from the south side by the steep hill that adjoins Beechen Cliff:

> "Or ever I cam to the Bridge of Bath that is over Avon I cam doun by a Rokky Hille fulle of fair Springes of Water: and on this Rokky Hille is sette a long streat as a Suburbe to the Cyte of Bath; and by this streate is a Chapelle of S. Mary Magdalen. Ther is a great gate with a Stone Arche at the Entre of the Bridge."

The Old Bath Bridge, demolished in the middle of the eighteenth century to make way for the present structure, consisted of "V fair Stone Arches". Having crossed this fine old bridge the traveller paused to observe:

> "Bytwixt the Bridge and the South Gate of Bath I markid fair Medowes on eche Hand, but especially on the lift Hond, and they ly South West of the Toun."

This gives a very clear impression of the strictly circumscribed limits of medieval Bath, a city almost entirely confined within the area of its walls and gates.

BATH

Leland's balanced judgment on Bath was infinitely more favourable than that of the Frenchman who associated it with the gates of Hell. The antiquary's appreciation of the city was, indeed, not unrelated to his approval of its plumbing facilities:

"The Cite of Bath is sette booth yn a fruteful and pleasant Botom, the which is environid on every side with greate Hilles out of the which cum many Springes of pure Water that be conveyid by dyverse ways to serve the Cite. Insomuch that Leade beyng made ther at hand many Houses yn the Toune have Pipes of Leade to convey Water from Place to Place."

Is it not delightful to find an inveterate medievalist like Leland ranking cleanliness next to godliness?

Once within the city and presumably washed and refreshed, Leland was free to observe that:

"There be 4 Gates yn the Toun by the Names of Est, West, North, and South."

which was the common arrangement of a medieval walled town.

Besides the cathedral and parish churches, what attracted Leland most in Bath were the city walls and the baths. There is a most vivid description of the city walls:

"The Toune Waulle within the Toune is of no great Highth to the yes: but without it is *a fundamentis* of a reasonable Highth and it stondith almost alle, lakking but a peace about Gascoyn's Tower. In the Walles of this tyme be no Tourres saving over the Toune Gate . . . There be divers notable Antiquitees engravid in stone that yet be sene yn the Walles of Bathe betwixt the South Gate and the West Gate: and agayn betwixt the West Gate and the North Gate. The first was an antique Hed of a man made al flat and having great Lokkes of Here as I have in a Coine of C. Antius. The Secunde that I did se bytwene the South and the North Gate was an Image, as I took it, of Hercules: for he held yn eche Hand a Serpent. Then I saw the Image of a foote man *vibrato gladio et praetenso clypeo*. Then I saw a Braunch with Leves foldid and wrethin into circles. Then I saw ii nakid Imagis lying a long, the one imbracing the other. Then I saw to antique Heddes with Heere as rofelid yn Lokkes. Then I saw a Grey-hound as renning and at the Taile of hym was a Stone engravid with great Romane Letters, but I could pike no sentence out of it. . . . Then I saw toward the West Gate an Image of a man embracid with 2 Serpentes. I took it for Laocoon. Betwixt the Weste and the North Gate I saw 2 Inscriptions, of the wich sum wordes were evident to the Reader, the Residew clene defacid. Then I saw the Image of a nakid Man. Then I saw a stone having *cupidines et labruscas intercurrentes*. Then I saw a Table having at eche Ende an Image vivid and florishid above and beneth. In this Table was an Inscription of a Tumbe or Burial wher in I saw playnly these wordes: *vixit annos XXX*. This inscription was meately hole but very diffusely written, as Letters for hole Wordes, and 2 or 3 Letters conveid in one. Then I saw 2 Images, wher of one was of a nakid Manne grasping a Serpent in eche Hand, as I tooke it: and this Image was not far from the North Gate."

Leland is very doubtful whether these inscriptions can have been placed in the walls of Bath by the Romans. He inclines to what certainly seems the more probable opinion, namely, that "they were gatherid of old Ruines ther, and sins set up in the Walles reedified in Testimonie of the antiquite of the Toun". A small portion of the medieval wall still stands along the street now called Borough Walls in the north-west of the city. But no inscriptions remain, and so much has the city risen in height since the Middle Ages that only the upper part of the old wall is still visible.

It is hard to say when the healing springs of Bath were resorted to again after the abandonment of the city by the Romans. Did the Anglo-Saxons discover the efficacy of the Bath waters? And did King Edgar diversify his coronation feastings with a health-cure? These questions are easy to pose: impossible to answer. We have, however, seen that gouty old gentlemen, sent by the King to end their days at the cathedral priory, embarrassed their hosts by an extreme longevity which can only be attributed to the healing springs. Leland, again, is our chief authority on the medieval baths. He observed that:

"There be 2 Springes of—whote Wather in the West South West Part of the Towne. Wher of the bigger is caullid the *Crosse Bath*, bycause it hath a Cross erectid in the midle of it. This Bath is much frequentid of People diseasid with Lepre, Pokkes, Scabbes, and great Aches, and is temperate and pleasant, having 11 or 12 Arches of Stone in the sides for men to stonde under yn tyme of Reyne. Many be holp by this Bathe from Scabbes and Aches. The other Bathe is a 2 hunderith Foote of, and is lesse in Cumpace withyn the Waulle then the other, having but 7 Arches yn the Waulle. This is caullid the *Hote Bathe*; for at cumming into it Men think that it wold scald the Flesch at the first, but after that the Flesch ys warmid and it is more tolerable and pleasaunt. Both these Bathes be in the midle of a lite Streat, and joine to S. John's Hospital: so that it may be thought that Reginalde Bishop of Bathe made this Hospitale nere there 2 commune Bathes to socour poore people resorting to them. The *Kinges Bathe* is very faire and large standing almost in the midle of the Toune, and at the West End of the Cathedrale Chirch. The Area that this Bath is yn is cumpassid with an high Stone Waulle. The Brimmes of this Bath hath a litle Walle cumpasing them, and in this Waul be 32 Arches for Men and Women to stand separately yn. To this Bath do Gentilmen resort. Ther goith a sluse out of this Bath, and servid in Tymes past with Water derivid out of it 2 Places in Bath Priorie usid for Bathes: els voide; for in them be no springes. The Colour of the Water of the Baynes is as it were a depe blew Se Water, and rikith like a sething Potte continually, having sumwhat a sulphureous and sumwhat a pleasant flavor. The Water that rennith from the 2 smaul Bathes goit by a Dike into Avon by West bynethe the Bridge. The Water that goith from the *Kinges Bath* turnith a Mylle, and after goith into Avon above Bath Bridge. In all the 3 Bathes a Man may evidently se how the Water burbelith up from the Springes."

This seems to show that the hot springs of Bath were tolerably well known in the Middle Ages and frequented by victims of "Lepre, Pokkes, Scabbes, and great Aches" and other persevering valetudinarians. But they did not have the international reputation which they enjoyed under the Roman occupation or at a much later date under the absolute monarchy of Beau Nash.

The prevailing impression of medieval Bath, then, is of an episcopal and monastic city which also enjoyed a certain national and local reputation for its healing springs. To the ordinary visitor the ecclesiastical tone and character of the city would have been most evident: something of the atmosphere that still pervades the Closes at Salisbury and Wells and lives in Anthony Trollope's novels. Nothing could be a greater contrast to what Bath was to become in the glittering reign of fashion and folly inaugurated by one who is commemorated in the Abbey Church as the Arbiter of Elegance.

7   Bath Abbey: the West Front, floodlit

"These walls, adorned with monument and bust,
Shew how Bath waters served to lay the dust."

8   The Abbey Nave in 1820, from an Engraving after Mackenzie

3

Tudor and Stuart Bath

THE AGE OF THE RENAISSANCE AND THE REFORMATION IS A time of dramatic and poignant interest in the history of Bath, as in the general story of England and Europe. It begins, appropriately enough, with an achievement in every way typical of the life and vigour of the early Renaissance: the rebuilding of the cathedral church in a manner typical of that age of rapid change and new adventurous ideas. This new creation—for it was no less—was principally inspired by two men: the bishop and the prior of Bath. The idea probably originated when Bishop Oliver King visited his cathedral priory in 1500 and found it in a lamentable state of moral and material decay. The church was falling to ruins, almsgiving was sadly neglected, while the monks were giving themselves over to all manner of excess in food and drink. So the bishop determined to stop the rot by laying his axe firmly to the tree of corruption. He addressed a series of injunctions to the priory which made provision for a wholesale rationalization of the finances of the house. In future the prior was to content himself with an income of £80 a year and the whole community of monks was to receive the same amount for their annual expenditure. When all allowance for food, drink, clothing, estate management, and other expenses had been made, a substantial balance was still left in hand to be spent on the repair of the church.

Now in 1499 William Bird, who had gained previous knowledge of the fabric of the church as sacrist of the monastery, was elected prior of Bath. The little we know of him suggests a man of high character and a ruler of great energy and ability. He and Oliver King—the reforming prior and the reforming bishop—proved to be an ideal combination. They worked perfectly in harness together and most truly laid the foundations of their great enterprise: the cathedral church of Bath that, with few subsequent alterations, stands to-day as a witness to their joint labours.

BATH

A pretty tale is told by Sir John Harington of how Bishop Oliver King conceived the plan of his new cathedral church.

"Lying at Bathe, and musing or meditating one night late after his devotions and prayers for the prosperity of Henry the Seventh and his children (who were then all or most part lyving), to which King he was principal Secretary and by him preferred to his bishoprick; he saw, or supposed he saw, a vision of the Holy Trynitie, with angells ascending and descending by a ladder, neer to the foote of which there was a fayre Olive tree, supporting a crowne, and a voyce that said—*Let an OLIVE establish the Crowne, and let a KING restore the Church.* Of this dreame or vision he took exceeding great comfort and told it to divers of his friends, applying it to the King his master in parte, and some parte to himselfe. To his master, because the Olive being the emblem or hieroglifick of peace and plentie, seemed to him to allude to King Henry VIIth, who was worthely counted the wisest and most peaceable King in all Europe of that age. To himself (for the wisest will flatter themselves somtime), because he was not only a chiefe counsellor to this King, and had bene his ambassador to conclude the most honourable peace with Charles the Eighth who paid (as Holinshed wryteth) 745 thousand ducketts, beside a yearly tribute of 25,000 crowns; but also he carried both the Olive and the King in his own name; and therefore thought he was specially designed for this church-worke, to the advauncement of which he had an extraordinary inclynation."

Later, Harington observes that at the west end of the church Bishop King "caused a representation to be graved of this his vision of the Trynitie, the angells, and the ladder; and on the north side the olive and crown"—which to this very day still puzzle the uninitiated visitor who is inclined to view the sculpture as an oblique allusion to Jacob's Ladder.

Although Bishop Oliver King died in 1503—some three years after the foundation of his great project—his immediate successors in the see continued his work and were actively assisted by the priors of Bath. Leland was informed when he visited Bath in 1540 that "Oliver King, bishop of Bath, began of late dayes a right goodly new chirch at the west part of the old chirch of St. Peter and finished a great part of it. The residue

36

was syns made by the prior of Bath, and especially by Gibbes the last prior ther that spent a grete summe of mony on that fabrike. Oliver King let almost al the old chirch of St. Peter's in Bath to go to ruine; the walls yet stand." This would seem to indicate that the rebuilding of the church was practically completed when the priory was dissolved at the end of the fourth decade of the century. Prior William Bird lived till 1525 and his exquisite chantry with its carved cornice and cresting of birds, begun some ten years before his death, is a fitting memorial of one who shone like a beacon-light in an age when monasticism was manifestly in decline.

Bishop King and Prior Bird, seeing how greatly the numbers of the monastic community had dwindled since the time of John of Tours, decided to restrict their new building to the nave-space of the previous church. The work was begun at the east end and gradually proceeded westward. The style is perpendicular with strong Renaissance influence and affinities to St. George's Chapel at Windsor, where Oliver King had been a canon. The light which pours through the tall and graceful windows has given the church the title of "the Lantern of England". It is one of the last great achievements of Catholic England. The eye ascends the fine proportions of nave and choir to alight upon the crowning glory of Bath Abbey: its fan-vaulting. St. George's, Windsor, and King's College Chapel, Cambridge, alone can compare with Bath in the excellence of this feature, one of the most beautiful art-forms evolved by the fertile genius of the Middle Ages.

We know something of the master-masons who undertook the technical direction of the building operations. Edward Leycester, possibly of the Corsham family of that name, filled this rôle at first and lived until 1527. He was succeeded by John Multon, described as a "freemason", one of those master craftsmen whose name has since been appropriated for other and more secret rites. In recent years, owing to the devoted labours of Knoop and Jones, these master-masons of the Middle Ages have become known to us. Richly do they deserve to be known, as their work has outlived the nicest designs of Kings and statesmen.

When Henry VIII set about his monstrous scheme of making the Church of Christ a department of the State, it was clear to

all at Bath that the days of the cathedral priory were numbered.
For the monasteries were veritable bulwarks of Catholicism
and the Holy See, and their wealth had far too great an attraction for a monarch whose avarice and rapacity knew no bounds.
In the summer of 1535 Dr. Richard Layton, one of the more
notorious of Thomas Cromwell's commissioners, visited Bath
Priory and sent the following report to his master:

"Hit may please yor goodnes to understande that we have
visited Bathe. Wheras we found the prior a right vertuose man
and I suppose no better of his cote, a man simple and not of the
greteste wit; his monkes worse then I have any fownde yet
both in bugerie and adulterie, sum one of them haveyng 10
women, some 8, and the reste so fewer. The house well repaired
but foure hundreth powndes in dett." All who are blessed with
the gift of common sense or have had occasion to examine the
principles on which Cromwell's commissioners composed the
Black Book, will recognize this story for what it is worth:
mendacious nonsense. Dr. Layton went on to tell Cromwell
that "The prior of Bathe hath sent unto yowe for a tokeyn a
leisse of Yrisshe Laners brede in a selle of hys in Yrelonde; no
harder hawkers can be, as he saythe."

But clearly a gift of Irish hawks was not going to appease one
who has acquired unenviable fame as *the Hammer of the Monks*:
especially when Dr. Layton accompanied the gift with his own
"discovery", if such an euphemism may be used to dignify plain
theft. "Ye shalle receve a bowke of Our Lades Miracles well
able to matche the Canterberie Tailles. Suche a bowke of dremes
as ye never sawe wich I fownde in the librarie." Two years
later the monks made a last desperate effort to purchase the
good-will of Thomas Cromwell by granting him an annuity of
£5 a year[1]. But the monastic wealth was not to be redeemed at
such a price, and so the monks bowed to the inevitable. Not,
however, without a final piece of subterfuge which did much to
rob the oppressors of their coveted spoils. On the very eve of
the Dissolution the monks sold or granted out many of their
lands on long-term leases and did the same with their advowsons
and rights to the revenues of benefices. In short, they did their
utmost to capitalise their revenues and at the same time to win

[1] Perhaps worth about £100 in our present money.

9   The Interior of the Abbey Church in 1806, showing the fine Renaissance
fittings, now discarded: from the plate by J. C. Nattes

10 The Montague Monument in the Nave of the Abbey Church: from a
lithograph after C. J. Richardson

themselves friends in the neighbourhood by creating these economic ties. The result was that, when on 27 January 1539 Drs. Tregonwell and Petre came to Bath to receive the formal surrender of the priory, these gentlemen found that the bulk of the monastic property had been disposed of by the monks on terms which they could not dishonour without arousing the hostility of the local gentry who were the chief beneficiaries of these transactions. So the monks raised their lump sums of cash for future needs and the commissioners had no alternative but to confirm the long-term leases to the country gentry.

The deed of surrender was signed by the prior, the sub-prior, the prior of Dunster (a dependent cell of Bath priory), and 18 monks. Only the most diehard of the "Romantic" school of historians now believe that the religious were turned out of their monasteries to fend for themselves in the world, to learn how to win a precarious living from the soil or the loom, or to throw themselves upon the charity of their neighbours. For it has now been established by the weightiest historical evidence that the great majority of monks either received substantial pensions or were provided to country livings and even more lucrative cures. This is precisely what happened at Bath. The prior William Holloway, *alias* Gibbes, received a pension of £80 a year (well over £1000 in our present money) and a house in Stall Street. The sub-prior was granted a pension of £9 a year, the next three monks in order of seniority got £8 a year, and all the others received annual pensions varying in value from £6 13s. 4d. to £4 13s. 4d. Several of the monks were later provided to livings in the neighbourhood of Bath. That these pensions were regularly paid seems to be fairly certain, as in 1553 nearly all the monks are mentioned by name in Cardinal Pole's pension list.

There is a sad story connected with William Holloway, the last prior, if we are to believe Thomas Charnock, the eccentric scholar who wrote a poem called *The Breviary of Natural Philosophy* in 1557. The prior, it appears, was highly versed in the somewhat esoteric chemical knowledge of his age, which called for familiarity with the Elixir of Life, the Philosopher's Stone, and other panaceas:

> "And now to obteyne thy purpose more rathe
> Let thy fire be as temperate as the Bath of the Bathe.
> Oh what a goodly and profitable Instrument
> Is the Bath of the Bathe for our fiery intent!
> To seeke all the World throughout I should not finde
> For profit and liberty a Fire more fitt to my minde.
> Goe or ride where you list for the space of a yeare,
> Thou needest not care for the mending of thy fire.
> A Monke of Bathe, which of that house was Pryor,
> Tould me in seacret he occupied none other fire;
> To whom I gave credit, even at the first season,
> Because it depended upon very good reason.
> He had our Stone, our Medicine, our Elixir, and all
> Which when the Abbie was supprest he hid in a wall:
> And ten dayes after he went to fetch it out,
> And there he found but the stople of a cloute."

Finding his precious chemical hocus-pocus stolen, the prior seems to have lost his reason and, like King Lear, to have wandered about the countryside blind and forlorn, accompanied by a small boy.

> "Then he told me he was in such an Agonie,
> That for the loss thereof he thought he should be frenzie;
> And a toy took him in the head to run such a race,
> That many a yeare after he had no setling place:
> And more, he is darke and cannot see,
> But hath a Boy to lead him through the country."

I confess that I find it hard to believe this story, which has a suspicious likeness to other tales of the same genre, but against my view I must set the almost contemporary date of the poem and its entire pointlessness unless founded in the realm of fact and not of fancy.

The disposal of the priory and its precinct affords an interesting glimpse into one aspect of the technique of the Dissolution. Cromwell's commissioners offered the church to the citizens of Bath for the sum of 500 marks, but "the townsmen, fearing if they bought it so cheape to be thought to cozin the King, so that the purchase might come under the compasse of the concealed lands, refused the proffer." The citizens then decided to take things into their own hands. They stripped the church of its glass and its iron, its bells and its lead, and then bargained with merchants for the sale of this plunder. Of the great cathedral church a mere skeleton, the bare walls and part of the roof, were left standing. This shell—for it was no more—together with buildings in the precinct and neighbouring lands, were then sold by Henry VIII to a certain Humphrey Colles. Before long Colles sold the site of the precinct and the bare church to Matthew Colthurst, whose son Edmund in 1560 presented "the carcass of St. Peter's Church" (as John Wood pictorially described the plundered abbey) to the citizens of Bath for their parish church. The rest of the precinct was sold in 1569 to Fulk Morley, through whose various descendants it came to the Duke of Kingston and Earl Manvers. It remains to add that the church of Bath sundered its special connection with the bishop of the diocese in 1543, when an act was passed making the dean and chapter of Wells the sole chapter for the bishopric of Bath and Wells. This arrangement has lasted to the present day, with Bath still taking formal precedence in the title of the see.

All through the long reign of Queen Elizabeth a great part of the church of Bath lay in a state of ruin and disrepair. Several attempts, it is true, were made to do something to the structure. In 1572 Peter Chapman, a soldier who had seen service in France and the Low Countries, paid for the repair of the east end of the north aisle. Soon afterwards the Queen's letters patent authorised collections to be made for seven years in every part of the kingdom for the rebuilding of the Church. This enabled a timber roof to be erected over the east, the north, and some of the south part of the fabric. It also led to the roofing and flooring of the tower. A little later the uppermost windows in the north wall of the choir were glazed, but it was not until the Spanish Armada had been fought and defeated that further progress was made with the choir so that services could be celebrated there. It was then thought fit to reconsecrate the church and to dedicate it to SS. Peter and Paul. But the south part of the transept and most of the nave were still unroofed and remained in this state until the accession of James I in 1603 when a certain Mr. Bellot, who had already contributed liberally to the fabric fund, gave a further £200 for the completion of the transept. Even then the sorry situation of the church may be judged by Sir John Harington's account of the work of Bishop Oliver King:

6   41

"Thus speedily it was pull'd down, but how slow it hath rysen again I may blush to wryte. Collections have bene made over all England, with which the chauncell is covered with blew slate, and an alms-house built *ex abundantia*; but the whole body of the Church stands bare *ex humilitate*. The rest of the money never comming to the townsmen's hands is laid up (as I suppose) with the money collected for Paul's steeple, which I leave to a *melius inquirendum*. And thus the Church lies still, like the poore traveller mentioned in the 10th of Luke, spoiled and wounded by thieves. The Priest goes by, the Levites go by, but doe nothing: only a good Samaritan, honest Mr. Billet[1] (worthy to be *billeted* in the New Jerusalem) hath powr'd some oyle in the wounds and maintained it in life."

The real restorer of the church of Bath was Bishop James Montague who ruled the see of Bath and Wells from 1608 to 1616. Sir John Harington, the godson and kinsman of Queen Elizabeth, who lived at Kelston, near Bath, and who has acquired immortal fame as the inventor of the water-closet, tells us a story of how this came to pass. When the bishop was at Bath on his primary visitation of the diocese he was suddenly caught in a violent shower which induced him, on Sir John's invitation, to seek shelter in the church. With admirable astuteness the knight led the bishop to the north aisle of the nave, which was still without a roof and offered little security from the storm. The bishop very naturally objected that they were still in the rain. "How can that be," asked Sir John, "seeing that we are within the Church?" "True," replied the prelate, "but your Church is unroofed, Sir John." "The more is the pity," rejoined the knight, "and the more doth it call for the munificence of your lordship." Whereupon the bishop applied himself at once to the restoration of the fabric, which was completed during his short episcopate at a cost of £1000. We may see his effigy there to-day on the north side of the nave, carefully described for us by Bloxham about a hundred years ago: "He is represented wearing a skull cap on his head, his chin is bearded and over his upper lip is the moustache, while round his neck is a ruff. He is vested in the rochet with full sleeves cuffed at the wrists. Over this appears the mantle of the Order of the Garter . . . connected in front of

---

[1] The pun demands that Mr. Bellott's name be thus spelt.

the neck by a cordon with pended tassels. On the left shoulder is the badge of the Order of the Garter. His head reposes on a cushion, and the hands are upheld vertically in prayer. Neither chimere or tippet are now apparent, but the effigy, which is sculptured in alabaster, has been denuded of the paint with which it was originally covered and in doing so a great mistake was made, for in removing the paint, that episcopal habit, the chimere, which ought to have been sculptured but was scamped and only painted in, has entirely disappeared. I have a simple notice of it taken by me in 1841: the chimere was then visible and the mantle appeared of a black or purple colour." Bishop Montague appears in effigy, as he was in real life, a typical Jacobean prelate, prudent and far-sighted: one of that sterling body of men portrayed by Dr. David Mathew in his vivid and penetrating study of *The Jacobean Age*. Through his arresting monument Bishop Montague has become well known to all Bathonians, with whom his name is a household word.

One of the principal effects of the Reformation and the dissolution of the cathedral priory on the life of Bath was a great increase in the power of the city authorities: the mayor and aldermen and the common council. Queen Elizabeth, who visited the city on at least two occasions, granted the citizens a charter in 1590 which contained very extensive privileges. Bath was declared to be a sole city of itself and the citizens to be a body corporate and politic by the name of mayor, aldermen, and citizens. Full powers of government were accorded to them and the area of the city, closely defined in the charter, was considerably enlarged. Hitherto the area of the city had been limited to the acreage within the four walls. Now it was extended to include the whole of the Barton farm to the north-west, the adjacent lands of the dissolved priory, and a large part of the parish of Walcote. The accounts of the chamberlain of the city, which have been printed for the years 1568–1602 by the Somerset Record Society, give a fascinating picture of the *minutiae* of city life in the sixteenth century. They show quite plainly, in the words of the editor, that "the Corporation was in undisputed possession of the city and they appeared to regulate all matters secular and spiritual": a remarkable contrast to the centuries in which the life of Bath was dominated by the bishop and his community of Benedictine monks.

We have given Leland's impression of the baths in the first half of the sixteenth century. Other writers in the later Tudor and Stuart periods have left vivid accounts of the somewhat primitive bathing amenities. Dr. William Turner, who was Dean of Wells and chief physician to King Edward VI, wrote in 1562 a treatise on the baths of England, Germany, and Italy which makes it very clear that the rich and the fashionable had little use for Bath: they preferred to visit foreign health resorts where the arts of Æsculapius were mixed with less innocent pleasures. Thomas Lupton, a minor poet of the time, is left lamenting:

> "How many use to Bathes abrode
> Far hence with cost to range
> Whereby they may their lothsome Lims
> To helthful Members change."

This period, however, saw the first attempt at a scientific treatise on the Bath waters. Its author was a certain Dr. John Jones who gave his book the quaint title of *The Bathes of Bathes Ayde*. He was, of course, a Welshman and a century later one who followed in his wake, Dr. Guidott, wrote about this pioneer work as follows:

"About the same time also one John Jones, an honest Cambro-Briton, frequenting the Baths for Practice, composed a little treatise on them, which he calls *Bath's Aid*, in which are some Things not contemptible, though in a Plain Country Dress, and which might satisfy and gratify the Appetite of those Times, which fed more heartily and healthily too on good Beef and Bag Pudding, than we do now upon Kickshaws and Haut-gusts; yet nothing of the true Nature is there discovered, only, as in almost all former Writers of Baths, chiefly Catholick, a strong Stench of Sulphur, and a great ado about a Subterranean Fire, a fit resemblance of Hell, at least of Purgatory." A revealing commentary on the *odium theologicum* of our ancestors!

The visit of Anne of Denmark, the Queen of James I, to the healing springs of Bath in 1616 seems to have been a real turning-point in the history of the city and its baths. A new bath which had been constructed in 1597 by the beneficent Mr. Bellot (whom we have already met in connection with the restoration of the Abbey) was patronized by the Queen, although it had become customary for "the best people" to bathe in the Cross Bath. The explanation vouchsafed by local tradition for Her Majesty's decision is that, when she was about to bathe, a flame of fire like a candle arose from the bottom of the cistern which so frightened her that, despite all the reassurances of the doctors, she refused to bathe there, but went to the new bath which has since borne her name and is known to-day as the Queen's Bath. From the day of Anne of Denmark's visit Bath was on the up-grade. Noble and aristocratic visitors, who had hitherto sought a health-cure and *divertissement* on the Continent, began to transfer their attention to Bath and to frequent its healing waters. With these persons of taste and fashion came a riff-raff of aspiring upstarts and vulgar intruders whose conduct has been unsparingly described by John Wood, the creator of the architectural glory of Bath:

"The Baths were like so many Bear Gardens, and Modesty was entirely shut out of them; People of both Sexes bathing by Day and Night naked; and Dogs, Cats, and even human creatures were hurl'd over the rails into the water, while People were bathing in it." Such was the nemesis of Anne of Denmark's visit. In the train of royalty, the mob. Or, as a later generation might well have inspired Anne to remark: "*Après nous, le déluge*". Queen Henrietta Maria, the refined and cultivated consort of Charles I, flatly refused to participate in these orgies and, when advised to take a cure, moved with her court to the French spa of Bourbon.

But the scruples of Henrietta Maria did not for long arrest the rising sun of Bath. In the reign of Charles II, with its relaxed moral tempo and its conscious reaction against the rule of Major-Generals and Saints, Bath recovered that status as a centre of fashionable society which Anne of Denmark's visit had initiated. Charles II and his Court were there in 1663. The object of their visit was of no small importance. It was an attempt to find in the mineral springs a remedy for the sterility of Queen Catherine of Braganza. A vast concourse of people accompanied the Merry Monarch and his Queen to the baths. Unfortunately the main purpose of their visit was not realized. Catherine could find no cure and her husband's paternal instincts found expression elsewhere.

From the Restoration period may be dated the preparation for Bath's unique position in English society in the eighteenth century. Scientists, not all of whom were entirely disinterested in the financial implications of their allotted task, "boosted" the healing properties of the Bath waters in fervent rhapsodies. The King's own physician, Sir Alexander Frayser, lent the seal of his approval to this publicity campaign and recommended the waters of Bath for drinking as well as for bathing. "From this period", Wood truly observes, "the drinking of the hot waters of Bath may be very justly said to have been established; and from the same period the trade of the city began to turn from the woollen manufacture to that of entertaining the strangers that came to it for the use of hot waters." The French historian of Bath, M. Barbeau, is even more emphatic. "This visit of Charles II's" he writes, ". . . inaugurated a new era. The character of the town was transformed; the new Bath, the Bath of the eighteenth century, began to manifest itself."

Before we leave seventeenth-century Bath it will be as well to gain a picture of the city as seen through the eyes of two experienced travellers: Samuel Pepys and Celia Fiennes. The famous diarist arrived at Bath with his wife and two friends on the evening of 12 June, 1668. They had no sooner found lodgings than they proceeded to the baths. "They are not as large as I expected, but yet pleasant; and the town most of stone, and clean, though the streets generally narrow." Satisfied, but somewhat weary, Pepys went to bed without supper and was up again very early next morning.

"Up at four o'clock, being by appointment called up to the Cross Bath, where we were carried one after another, myself, and wife, and Betty Turner, Willet, and W. Hewer. And by and by, though we designed to have done before company come, much company come; very fine ladies; and the manner pretty enough, only methinks it cannot be clean to go so many bodies together in the same water. Good conversation among them that are acquainted here, and stay together. Strange to see how hot the water is; and in some places, though this is the most temperate bath, the springs so hot as the feet not able to endure. But strange to see, when women and men herein, that live all the season in these waters, that cannot but be parboiled, and look like the creatures of the bath! Carried away, wrapped in a sheet, and in a chair, home; and there one after another thus carried, I staying above two hours in the water, home to bed, sweating for an hour; and by and by comes musick to play to me, extraordinary good as ever I heard at London almost, or anywhere: 5 s."

On Sunday Pepys, like the good sober citizen he was at heart, made his way to the Abbey church.

"Up, and walked up and down the town, and saw a pretty good market-place, and many good streets, and very fair stone-houses. And so to the great Church, and there saw Bishop Montagu's tomb; and, when placed, did there see many brave people come, and, among others, two men brought in, in litters, and set down in the chancel to hear: but I did not know one face. Here a good organ; but a vain, pragmatical fellow preached a ridiculous, affected sermon, that made me angry."

Pepys went again to the Abbey for the evening service but had the mortification of seeing the same "vain pragmatical fellow" ascend the stairs of the pulpit. His reaction, inspired alike by experience and common sense, was peculiar neither to him nor to his age: "I slept most of the sermon"!

On Monday morning Pepys was up again early and visited the baths with his landlord "Up, and with Mr. Butts to look into the baths, and find the King and Queen's full of a mixed sort, of good and bad, and Cross only almost for the gentry." The same day Pepys and his companions left the city.

A very different type of traveller, with a woman's eye for small detail, was Celia Fiennes, who visited Bath in the reign of William and Mary about the year 1695. Like Pepys she lost no time in visiting the baths once she had found lodgings, and her graphic picture of the organization and customs of the bathing-establishment is the classic description of Bath in the age that immediately preceded the reign of Beau Nash.

"The wayes to the bath are all difficult, the town lyes Low in a bottom and its steep ascents all wayes out of the town. The houses are indifferent, the streetes of a good size well pitched.

There are severall good houses built for Lodgings that are new and adorned, and good furniture, the baths in my opinion makes the town unpleasant, the aire so low, encompassed with high hills and woods. There is 5 baths the hot bath the most hot springs—its but small and built all round, which makes it the hotter—out of it runns the water into a bath called the Le pours.

"The third bath is called the Cross bath which is some thing bigger than the former and not so hot; the Cross in the middle has seates round it for the Gentlemen to sitt, and round the walls are Arches with seates for the Ladyes, all stone and the seate is stone and if you thinke the seate is too Low they raise it with a Coushon as they call it, another Stone, but indeed the water bears you up that the seate seemes as easy as a down Coushon. Before the Arch the Ladyes use to have a laced toilet hung up on the top of the Arch and so to shelter their heads even to the water if they please. You Generally sit up to the Neck in water, this Cross bath is much the Coolest and is used mostly in the heate of summer; there are Gallery's round the top that the Company that does not Bathe that day walkes in and lookes over into the bath on their acquaintance and company —there are such a number of Guides to each bath of women to waite on the ladyes, and of men to waite on the Gentlemen, and they keepe their due distance. There is a serjeant belonging to the baths that all the bathing tyme walkes in galleryes and takes notice order is observed and punishes the rude, and most people of fashion sends to him when they begin to bathe, then he takes particular Care of them and Complements you every morning which deserves its reward at the end of the Season. When you would walk about the bath I use to have a woman guide or two to Lead me for the water is so strong it will quickly tumble you down, and then you have 2 of the men guides goes at a distance about the bath to Cleare the way. At the sides of the Arches are rings that you may hold by and so walke a little way, but the springs bubbles up so fast and so strong and are so hot up against the bottoms of ones feete, Especially in that they Call the Kitching in the bath, which is a great Cross with seates in the middle and many hot springs riseth there. The Kings bath is very large, as large as the rest put together, in it is the hot pumpe that persons are pumpt at for Lameness or on their heads for palsyes. I saw one pumpt, they put on a broad brim'd hatt with the Crown Cut out so as the brims Cast off the water from the face; they are pumpt in the bath, one of the men Guides pumps—they have two pence I thinke for 100 pumps. The water is scallding hot out of the pump, the armes or Legs are more easyly pumped. The Ladyes goes into the bath with Garments made of a fine yellow canvas, which is stiff and made large with great sleeves like a parsons gown; the water fills it up so that its borne off that your shape is not seen, it does not cling close as other linning, which Lookes sadly in the poorer sort that go in their own linning. The Gentlemen have drawers and wastcoates of the same sort of canvas, this is the best linning, for the bath water will Change any other yellow. When you go out of the bath you go within a doore that leads to Steps which you ascend by degrees that are in the water, then the doore is shut which shutts down into the water a good way, so you are in a private place where you still ascend severall more steps and let your Canvass drop of by degrees into the water, which your women guides take off, and the meane tyme your maides flings a garment of flannell made like a Nightgown with great sleeves over your head, and the guides take the taile and so pulls it on you Just as you rise the steps, and your other garment drops off so you are wrapped up in the flannell and your nightgown on the top, and your slippers and so you are set in Chaire which is brought into the roome which are called slips, and there are Chimney's in them, you may have fires. These are in severall parts of the sides of the bath for the Conveniency of persons going in and out of the bath decently, and at the top of the staires stands a woman that Layes a woollen Cloth for you to set your bare foot, and also to give you attendance. The Chaires you go in are a low seate and with frames round and over your head and all cover'd inside and out with red bayes and a Curtaine drawn before of the same which makes it Close and warme; then a Couple of men with staves takes and Carryes you to your lodging and sets you at your bedside where you go to bed and lye and sweate some tyme as you please. Your own maides and the maides of the house gets your fire and waites on you till you rise to get out of your sweate. All the baths has the same attendance, the queens bath is bigger then the other three but not and neare so big as the Kings, which do run into each other and is only parted by a wall and at one place a great arch where they run into each other. The queens bath is a degree hotter than the Cross bath and the Kings bath much hotter, these have all gallery's round and the pump is in one of these galleryes at the Kings bath which the Company drinks of, its very hot and tastes like the water that boyles Eggs, has such a smell, but the nearer the pumpe you drinke it, the hotter and less offencive and more spiriteous. The baths are all Emptyed as soone as the Company goes out, which is about 10 or 11 of the Clock in the morning; then by sluces they empty at once the bath so it fills againe. I have seen all the springs bubble up as thicke out of the ground when the baths have been empty. The bottom is gravell. So they will be full for the evening if Company would go in againe, if so they empty them againe at Night and they are filled against the morning and there will be such a white scum on the bath which the guides goes and scimms off Cleane before any Company goes in; if they go in while this scum is on it gives them the bath mantle as they call it, makes them breake out into heate and pimples; the like will be on them if they go into the bath before they have purged, especially in the hotter bath. The places for divertion about the bath is either the walkes in that they call the Kings Mead which is a pleasant green meaddow, where are walkes round and Cross it, no place for Coaches, and indeed there is little use of a Coach only to bring and Carry the Company from the bath for the wayes are not proper for Coaches.

"The town and all its accomodations is adapted to the bathe-ing and drinking of the waters and to nothing else, the streetes are well pitched and Cleane kept and there are Chaires as in London to Carry the better sort of people in visits, or if sick or infirme and is only in the town, for its so Encompassed with high hills few care to take the aire on them."

The impression, then, that one has of seventeenth-century Bath from contemporary records is that of a city rich in possi-bilities as a pleasure and health resort but lacking as yet in comforts and amenities. Besides bathing there was little to do but walk in the fields and play bowls : pastimes which made no

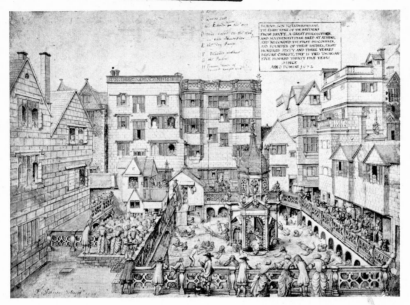

11   Restoration Bath: from a drawing by T. Johnson (*ca.* 1670)

12   Taking the Waters: from an engraving by J. C. Nattes

13, 14 Winter and Summer on the Kennet and Avon Canal, near Bath

great appeal to the *beau monde*. Dancing of a sort and horse-racing took place, especially when the city was favoured with a visitor such as the Duke of Grammont; but the former was often ill-arranged and little more than a formal excuse for the reign of licence. In short, what the city needed was a man of real organizing ability who could impose a strict regimen upon the motley crowds who thronged the streets and baths and places of amusement. The hour did not fail to produce the man.

4

The Bath of Beau Nash

A VERY MARKED IMPROVEMENT IN THE TONE AND MANNERS of English society may be observed at the end of the seventeenth century. This was one of the many blessings conferred on this country by the Glorious Revolution of 1688 in which "our canonized ancestors"—as Burke so rightly termed the Whig defenders of the constitution—gave the *coup de grâce* to Stuart absolutism. Once the constitution had been secured and the blessings of personal liberty had become the inalienable right of every Englishman, society was able to devote itself seriously to its own pleasures and amusements free from the haunting fear of revolution and civil war. The problem at once arose, where was fashionable society to foregather in the hot summer months? London was clearly intolerable during the period of warm weather; yet, as Goldsmith says:

"At this time London was the only theatre in England for pleasure or intrigue. A spirit of gaming had been introduced in the licentious age of Charles II, and had by this time thriven surprisingly. Yet all its devastations were confined to London alone. To this great mart of every folly, sharpers from every country daily arrived for the winter; but were obliged to leave the kingdom at the approach of summer, in order to open a new campaign at Aix, Spa, or the Hague. Bath, Tunbridge, Scarborough, and other places of the same kind here, were then frequented only by such as really went for relief: the pleasures they afforded were merely rural; the company splenetic, rustic, and vulgar. In this situation of things, people of fashion had no agreeable summer retreat from the town, and usually spent that season amidst a solitude of country squires, parsons' wives, and visiting tenants or farmers; they wanted some place where they might have each other's company, and win each other's money, as they had done during the winter in town."

The problem could not be stated with greater clarity. Given

52

THE BATH OF BEAU NASH

the absence of civil strife, the presence of political stability, and the rising tide of national prosperity, what were people of fashion to do during the summer months? Where were they to go?

The Crown is the natural apex and leader of English society, and it was Queen Anne herself who set the example by visiting Bath in 1702 and returning there in the following summer. Immense crowds of people followed their sovereign to Bath and amongst them was one who was destined to transform the ancient city beyond all recognition. The name of this person was Richard Nash, who became known familiarly to all succeeding generations as Beau Nash, the Arbiter of Elegance.

The career of this extraordinary man is fortunately known to us in some detail through the labours of Oliver Goldsmith, who wrote his life and seems to have enjoyed his personal friendship. This *Life of Richard Nash* is a primary source for the history of Bath in the eighteenth century and will serve as the basis of much of the account that follows. "The amours of coxcombs and the pursuits of debauchees", Goldsmith somewhat dubiously assumes, "are as destitute of novelty to attract us as they are of variety to entertain": and he hastily goes on to observe that "The life of Richard Nash is incapable of supplying any entertainment of this nature to a prurient curiosity". Be that as it may, it is indisputable that five men of exceptional qualities made eighteenth-century Bath what it was: Beau Nash, Dr. William Oliver, Ralph Allen, and the two Woods. Of these five the Beau has enjoyed the most enduring fame.

Richard Nash was born at Swansea in the autumn of 1674. His father, who was a partner in a glass manufactory, sent him to Carmarthen School, whence he proceeded to Jesus College, Oxford. His Oxford career foreshadowed all that was to come, for, alas! "in the neighbourhood of every university there are girls who with some beauty, some coquetry, and little fortune, lie upon the watch for every raw youth, more inclined to make love than to study. Our hero was quickly caught, and went through all the mazes and adventures of a college intrigue before he was seventeen: he offered marriage, the offer was accepted, but the whole affair coming to the knowledge of his tutors, his happiness, or perhaps his future misery, was prevented, and he was sent home from college, with necessary advice to him, and proper instructions to his father." Still offering libations on the altar of Love, the Beau decided to become a soldier, attracted by the glamour of the red uniform. He purchased his commission, but soon found the army irksome as certain practical duties were demanded of him which stood in the way of his social engagements. So Nash quitted the army and enrolled himself as a law student in the Middle Temple. Once again the demands of society took precedence over the obligations of study. The Beau found that he excelled in one thing only: the organization of social ceremonies. A golden opportunity came for him when, on the accession of William of Orange, the Templars wished to display their loyalty to His Majesty. A magnificent ceremony of welcome was arranged by the Beau which prompted the monarch to offer him a knighthood. This he had the good sense to decline. But his name was made. He consorted freely with the "best society" and his taste and elegance became a by-word for the *beau monde*.

How did the Beau maintain himself financially? There is only one answer. By gambling. He was a professional gamester and it was his "profession" that drove him to Bath in the wake of Queen Anne in 1702. Within a very short time he became the Uncrowned King of Bath, the Arbiter of Elegance, and the Dictator of the manners of Polite Society. This triumph he achieved by sheer force of personality. For though, as Goldsmith says, he was by birth "placed in the middle rank of life" he yet "had too much merit not to become remarkable", even if he had "too much folly to arrive at greatness". In appearance he was singular and arresting, though not particularly attractive. "He always wore a white hat; and, to apologize for this singularity, said he did it purely to secure it from being stolen; his dress was tawdry, though not perfectly genteel; he might be considered a Beau of several generations, and in his appearance he in some measure mixed the fashions of the last age with those of the present. He perfectly understood elegant expense, and generally passed his time in the very best company, if persons of the first distinction deserve that title." The success of this "sweet and lovable creature", as Miss Edith Sitwell calls him, was, I repeat, a triumph of forceful personality. This, allied

15   Beau Nash: from the painting by William Hoare in the Pump Room

16   The Old Bath Bridge: from a plate by W. Watts (1819)

with his consummate powers of organization, made him King of Bath and Dictator of the *Beau Monde.*

When Beau Nash arrived at Bath on the occasion of Queen Anne's visit he found a certain Captain Webster playing the part of Master of Ceremonies. This man, like the Beau, was a professional gamester, but without the Beau's varied social accomplishments. True he had had the good sense to organize weekly balls at the town-hall of Bath, charging each man half-a-guinea for these improved amenities.

"Still, however" (says Goldsmith) "the amusements of this place were neither elegant, nor conducted with delicacy. General society among people of rank or fortune was by no means established. The nobility still preserved a tincture of Gothic haughtiness, and refused to keep company with the gentry at any of the public entertainments of the place. Smoking in the rooms was permitted; gentlemen and ladies appeared in a disrespectful manner at public entertainments in aprons and boots. With an eagerness common to those whose pleasures come but seldom, they generally continued them too long; and thus they were rendered disgusting by too free an enjoyment. If the company liked each other, they danced till morning; if any person lost at cards, he insisted on continuing the game till luck should turn. The lodgings for visitors were paltry though expensive; the dining-rooms and other chambers were floored with boards, coloured brown with soot and small-beer, to hide the dirt; the walls were covered with unpainted wainscot; the furniture corresponded with the meanness of the architecture; a few oak chairs, a small looking-glass, with a fender and tongs, composed the magnificence of these temporary habitations. The city was in itself mean and contemptible; no elegant buildings, no open streets, nor uniform squares!"

Within a short time Nash won the confidence of Captain Webster and assumed the rôle of an aide-de-camp. Then Captain Webster was killed in a duel by a man who had lost heavily while playing cards with him, and Beau Nash stepped naturally and easily into his place as Master of the Ceremonies.

The first steps that the Beau took to improve the amenities at Bath and so to attract the world of fashion were of a very practical nature. He placed the pump room in charge of a special official called the pumper who paid a yearly rent to the corporation. The streets of the city were properly paved, lighted, and cleaned and the insolence of the chairmen was repressed by severe penalties. Special privileges were granted to invalids who came to bathe or drink the waters at Bath and the lodging-houses and promenades were improved beyond recognition. Above all, the Beau realized the sweet attractive power of music and the value of polished and well-regulated entertainment. He therefore promoted a subscription for a band of six trained musicians paid at the rate of a guinea a week. At the same time a certain Thomas Harrison, at the Beau's behest, built a set of handsome Assembly Rooms close to the South Parade, where the company might foregather of an evening for a variety of entertainments.

Having in this manner freed Bath from its rustic associations and its primitive amenities, the Beau proceeded to draw up a *Code of Behaviour* for visitors that has since acquired something like world fame. The rules of the King of Bath were put up in the pump room for all to see:

RULES TO BE OBSERVED AT BATH

1. "That a visit of ceremony at first coming, and another at going away, are all that is expected or desired by ladies of quality and fashion,—except impertinents."

2. "That ladies coming to the ball appoint a time for their footmen coming to wait on them home, to prevent disturbance and inconvenience to themselves and others."

3. "That gentlemen of fashion never appearing in a morning before the ladies in gowns and caps, show breeding and respect."

4. "That no person take it ill that any one goes to another's play or breakfast, and not theirs;—except captious by nature."

5. "That no gentleman give his ticket for the balls to any but gentlewomen.—N.B.: Unless he has none of his acquaintance."

6. "That gentlemen crowding before the ladies at the ball, show ill-manners; and that none do so for the future,—except such as respect nobody but themselves."

7. "That no gentleman or lady take it ill that another dances before them;—except such as have no pretence to dance at all."

17   The Circus: from a plate by A. Woodroffe (*ca.* 1820)

THE BATH OF BEAU NASH

8. "That the elder ladies and children be content with a second bench at the ball, as being past or not come to perfection."

9. "That the younger ladies take notice how many eyes observe them.—N.B.: This does not extend to the Have-at-alls."

10. "That all whisperers of lies and scandal be taken for their authors."

11. "That all repeaters of such lies and scandal be shunned by all company,—except such as have been guilty of the same crime. N.B.: Several men of no character, old women and young ones of questioned reputation, are great authors of lies in these places, being of the sect of levellers."

"These laws", Goldsmith tells us, "were written by Mr. Nash himself, and by the manner in which they are drawn up he undoubtedly designed them for wit." "But" (he hastens to add) "Nash was not born a writer; for whatever humour he might have in conversation, he used to call a pen his torpedo: whenever he grasped it, it benumbed all his faculties."

Not content with transforming the social amenities of the city and legislating for the world of fashion, Beau Nash established himself as a dictator of manners, whose laws and commands brooked no disobedience. On three things he was peculiarly insistent: that duelling and the wearing of swords should be totally suppressed, that women should cease to appear at assemblies dressed in white aprons, and that men should never appear at these fashionable gatherings in riding-boots. In the matter of duelling Nash took drastic measures. Whenever he heard of a challenge given or accepted he immediately had both parties arrested. He forbade the wearing of swords in Bath under the strictest censures, and gradually, under his dictatorship, the practice of duelling dwindled and finally died out altogether. This was an impressive advance in civilized behaviour, as what men were forbidden to do in Bath they soon had no wish to do in London or elsewhere. The fight against white aprons was sharp and severe. The climax came when the Duchess of Queensberry appeared at an assembly in an apron which the Beau ruthlessly stripped from her and threw among her ladies-in-waiting, observing that none but Abigails appeared in white aprons. The duchess took the insult in very good part and meekly submitted to the Arbiter of Elegance. Nash had a

8

57

devastating way of dealing with men who appeared at the assemblies in boots. He would go up to an offender and ask him in an arch manner whether he had "forgot his horse". But the country squires were slow to yield obedience to the King of Bath. So Nash, being obliged to supplement sarcasm by ridicule, composed a song which he called *Frontinella's Invitation to the Assembly*:

> "Come, one and all, to Hoyden Hall,
>   For there's the assembly this night;
>   None but prude fools
>   Mind manners and rules;
>   We Hoydens do decency slight.
>   Come, trollops and slatterns,
>   Cocked hats and white aprons,
>   This best our modesty suits;
>   For why should not we
>   In dress be as free
>   As Hogs-Norton squires in boots?"

This engaging jingle appears to have had the desired effect, for after a time riding-boots followed the way of white aprons and were no more to be seen at the Bath assemblies.

If we wish to gain a swift impression of the social round at Bath, we cannot better than follow Oliver Goldsmith, who dwells on the pleasures of the city with an obvious relish:

"Upon a stranger's arrival at Bath he is welcomed by a peal of the Abbey Bells, and, in the next place, by the voice and music of the city waits. For these civilities, the ringers have generally a present made them of half-a-guinea, and the waits of half-a-crown, or more, in proportion to the person's fortune, generosity, or ostentation. These customs, though disagreeable, are however, liked or they would not continue. The greatest incommodity attending them is the disturbance the bells must give the sick. But the pleasure of knowing the name of every family that comes to town recompenses the inconvenience. Invalids are fond of news, and upon the first sound of the bells everybody sends out to inquire for whom they ring.

"After the family is thus welcomed to Bath, it is the custom for the master of it to go to the public places, and subscribe two guineas at the assembly-houses towards the balls and music in the pump-house, for which he is entitled to three tickets every

18 "A Real Scene on the Parade
at Bath"

19 "A Modern Belle going to the
Rooms at Bath"

20 The Parade, in the late Eighteenth Century

21   The Cross Bath : from the plate by J. C. Nattes (1806)

ball night. His next subscription is a crown, half-a-guinea, or a guinea, according to his rank and quality, for the liberty of walking in the private walks belonging to Simpson's assembly-house; a crown or half-a-guinea is also given to the booksellers, for which the gentleman is to have what books he pleases to read at his lodgings, and at the coffee-house another subscription is taken for pen, ink, and paper, for such letters as the subscriber shall write at it during his stay. The ladies, too, may subscribe to the booksellers, and to a house by the pump-room, for the advantage of reading the news, and for enjoying each other's conversation.

"Things being thus adjusted, the amusements of the day are generally begun by bathing, which is no unpleasing method of passing away an hour or so.

"The baths are five in number. On the south-west side of the Abbey Church is the King's Bath, which is an oblong square; the walls are full of niches, and at every corner are steps to descend into it: this bath is said to contain 427 tons and 50 gallons of water; and on its rising out of the ground over the springs, it is sometimes too hot to be endured by those who bathe therein. Adjoining to the King's Bath, there is another, called the Queen's Bath; this is of a more temperate warmth, as borrowing its water from the other.

"In the south-west part of the city are three other baths, viz: the Hot Bath, which is not much inferior in heat to the King's Bath, and contains 53 tons, 2 hogsheads, and 11 gallons of water; the Cross Bath, which contains 52 tons, 3 hogsheads, and 11 gallons; and the Leper's Bath, which is not so much frequented as the rest.

"The King's Bath (according to the best observations) will fill in about nine hours and a half; the Hot Bath in about eleven hours and a half; and the Cross Bath in about the same time.

"The hours for bathing are commonly between six and nine in the morning, and the baths are every morning supplied with fresh water; for when the people have done bathing, the sluices in each bath are pulled up, and the water is carried off by drains into the River Avon.

"In the morning the lady is brought in a close chair, dressed in her bathing clothes, to the bath; and, being in the water, the

woman who attends presents her with a little floating dish like a basin; into which the lady puts a handkerchief, a snuff-box, and a nosegay. She then traverses the bath; if a novice, with a guide; if otherwise, by herself; and having amused herself thus while she thinks proper, calls for her chair, and returns to her lodgings.

"The amusement of bathing is immediately succeeded by a general assembly of people at the pump-room; some for pleasure, and some to drink the hot waters. Three glasses at three different times is the usual portion for every drinker; and the intervals between every glass are enlivened by the harmony of a small band of music, as well as by the conversation of the gay, the witty, or the forward.

"From the pump-room the ladies, from time to time, withdraw to a female coffee-house, and from thence return to their lodgings to breakfast. The gentlemen withdraw to their coffee-houses, to read the papers, or converse on the news of the day, with a freedom and ease not to be found in the metropolis.

"People of fashion make public breakfasts at the assembly-houses, to which they invite their acquaintances, and they sometimes order private concerts; or, when so disposed, attend lectures on the arts and sciences, which are frequently taught there in a pretty superficial manner, so as not to tease the understanding, while they afford the imagination some amusement. The private concerts are performed in the ball-rooms; the tickets a crown each.

"Concert breakfasts at the assembly-houses sometimes make also a part of the morning's amusement here, the expenses of which are defrayed by a subscription among the men. Persons of rank and fortune who can perform are admitted into the orchestra, and find a pleasure in joining with the performers.

"Thus we have the tedious morning fairly over. When noon approaches, and church (if any please to go there) is done, some of the company appear upon the parade, and other public walks, where they continue to chat and amuse each other, till they have formed parties for the play, cards, or dancing for the evening. Another part of the company divert themselves with reading in the booksellers' shops, or are generally seen taking the air and exercise, some on horseback, some in coaches. Some walk in the meadows round the town, winding along the side of the River Avon and the neighbouring canal; while others are seen scaling some of those romantic precipices that overhang the city.

"When the hour of dinner draws nigh, and the company are returned from their different recreations, the provisions are generally served with the utmost elegance and plenty. Their mutton, butter, fish, and fowl, are all allowed to be excellent, and their cookery still exceeds their meat.

"After dinner is over, and evening prayers ended, the company meet a second time at the pump-house. From this they retire to the walks, and from thence go to drink tea at the assembly-houses, and the rest of the evenings are concluded either with balls, plays, or visits. A theatre was erected in the year 1705, by subscription, by people of the highest rank, who permitted their arms to be engraven on the inside of the house, as a public testimony of their liberality towards it. Every Tuesday and Friday evening is concluded with a public ball, the contributions to which are so numerous, that the price of each ticket is trifling. Thus Bath yields a continued rotation of diversions, and people of all ways of thinking, even from the libertine to the methodist, have it in their power to complete the day with employments suited to their inclinations."

At all these pleasures and pursuits Beau Nash was supreme arbiter: the uncrowned King of Bath whose word was unalterable law. Even princesses of the blood royal had no power over him. Thus when Princess Amelia, the daughter of George II, asked for one dance more when Nash had given the signal for the music to stop at 11 o'clock, she was curtly informed by the Beau that the rules of Bath were as unalterable as those of Lycurgus and that nothing would induce him to grant her request. By virtue of this undeviating obedience to rule and precedent manners rapidly improved and soon reached a very high level of excellence. The *beau monde* flocked to Bath, certain that dignity would here prevail and that there could arise no occasion for scandal or outrage. Bath became the natural centre and rallying-point of Fashion and Polite Society as well as of Intelligence and Wit during the long months of summer. All the great names of the eighteenth century are to be found here. One has only to study the plaques studded so thickly on the houses of present-day Bath to realize that few who were famed in society, politics, or letters, failed to reside here at some period of their lives. And of Beau Nash, the presiding genius of this gay and brilliant society, we can say with Goldsmith that "He was the first who diffused a desire of society and an easiness of address among a whole people, who were formerly censured by foreigners for a reservedness of behaviour and an awkward timidity in their first approaches. He first taught a familiar intercourse among strangers at Bath and Tunbridge, which still subsists among them. That ease and open access first acquired there, our gentry brought back to the metropolis, and thus the whole kingdom by degrees became more refined by lessons originally derived from him." This was a great achievement. In truth, "We see a kingdom beginning with him, and sending off Tunbridge as one of its colonies."

The first four decades of the eighteenth century were the hey-day of Beau Nash's influence. Then his dominion underwent a decline: partly as a natural result of the onslaught of old age, partly as an outcome of the parliamentary legislation against gambling passed in the years 1739 and 1745. In his old age, if the truth be told, the Beau was frankly a bore. He had a tiresome habit of repeating his old jokes at great length: few of them stood up to such a test. He was constantly vexed by lawsuits and slanders, his fortunes declined, and he died in comparative poverty and neglect at the age of 87 on 12 February, 1761, at his house in St. John's Court.

The character of the Monarch of Bath has emerged, I hope, with sufficient clarity in the foregoing pages. To most of us to-day he would appear an insufferable snob, for he was always courting the company of those of royal and noble birth. He had, we must admit, considerable success. In 1738 Frederick, Prince of Wales, came to Bath and presented Nash with a large gold enamelled snuffbox. Nash returned the compliment and erected a handsome obelisk to the Prince in Queen Square, where it is to be admired to this day. The Prince of Orange displayed his favour to Nash in the same way and was rewarded with an obelisk in Orange Grove near the Abbey. It was all very delightful and edifying. The Earl of Chesterfield, however, who was a very frequent visitor to Bath, where he wrote some of his

22   The Interior of the Pump Room in 1806: from the plate by J. C. Nattes

23　The Pump Room and Colonnade

24　The Interior of the Concert Room
Both from Plates by J. C. Nattes (1806)

more celebrated letters, treated the Beau with some coldness and reserve. On the occasion when Nash's devotees placed a portrait of the Beau in Wiltshire's ballroom between the busts of Newton and Pope, the Earl was moved to write the following scornful epigram:

> "Immortal Newton never spoke
> More truth, than here you'll find,
> Nor Pope himself e'er penn'd a joke
> More cruel on mankind.
>
> The picture placed the busts between
> Gives satire its full strength;
> Wisdom and Wit are little seen,
> But Folly at full length."

Yet, when all is said, it is hard to dissent from Edith Sitwell's verdict that Nash was "a sweet and lovable creature". Generous to a fault, he was ever assisting others: preventing young men from falling victims to "gulls" and "rooks" and maidens from losing their good name and virtue to charlatans and mountebanks. He loathed hypocrisy and pride, as the following story of Goldsmith well illustrates:

"Nash and one of his friends, being newly arrived at Tunbridge from Bath, were one day on the walks, and, seeing a young fellow of fortune with whom they had some slight acquaintance, joined him. After the usual chat and news of the day was over, Mr. Nash asked him, how long he had been at the Wells and what company was there? The other replied, he had been at Tunbridge a month: but as for company, he could find as good at a Tyburn ball. Not a soul was to be seen, except a parcel of gamesters and strumpets, who would grant the last favour for a single stake at the Pharaoh bank. 'Look you there,' continued he, 'that goddess of midnight, so fine at t'other end of the walks, by Jove she was mine this morning for half a guinea; and she there, who brings up the rear with powdered hair and dirty ruffles, she's pretty enough, but cheap, perfectly cheap; why, my boys, to my own knowledge, you may have her for a crown and dish of chocolate into the bargain—last Wednesday night we were happy.' 'Hold there, sir,' cried the gentleman; 'as for your having the first lady, it is possible it may be true, and I intend to ask her about it, for she is my sister; but as to your being happy with the other last Wednesday, I am sure you are a lying rascal. She is my wife, and we came here but last night.' The buck vainly asked pardon; the gentleman was going to give him proper chastisement, when Mr. Nash interposed in his behalf, and obtained his pardon upon condition that he quitted Tunbridge immediately."

If his character and outlook were essentially trivial and super-ficial, uninfluenced by great designs and high principles—"too much merit not to become remarkable, yet too much folly to arrive at greatness", to repeat Goldsmith's well-known judgment —he was yet loved by many and hated by none. We leave him, then, with many lingering regrets, for though "Nature had by no means framed Mr. Nash for a *beau garçon*; his person was clumsy, too large and awkward, and his features harsh, strong, and peculiarly irregular; yet even with those disadvantages he made love, became a universal admirer of the sex, and was universally admired." When he died the citizens of Bath mourned as one man their Uncrowned King, gave him a hand-some funeral, and erected in the Abbey Church a fitting monu-ment to the Arbiter of Elegance:

> "Adeste O Cives, adeste Lugentes!
> Hic silent Leges
> RICARDI NASH, Armigeri
> Nihil amplius imperantis;
> Qui diu et utilissime
> Assumptus Bathoniae
> Elegantiae Arbiter,
> Eheu!
> Morti (ultimo designatori)
> Haud indecore succubuit.
> Anno Domini MDCCLXI Aetatis suae LXXXVII
> Beatus ille qui sibi imperiosus."

What could be stranger than to find the Arbiter of Elegance commemorated thus on the walls of a Benedictine Abbey! *O tempora! O mores!*

The second of the five remarkable men who co-operated in the creation of the greatness of Bath in the eighteenth century was the physician Dr. William Oliver. Of Cornish origin and the son of a doctor of the same name who had built up a modest practice

25, 26   Bath from the Avon: from plates by J. C. Nattes

27   Dr. Oliver and Jerry Pierce examining Patients: from the painting by William Hoare in the
Royal Mineral Water Hospital

at Bath, William Oliver was educated at the Universities of Cambridge and Leyden and spent the early years of his professional life at Plymouth. About the year 1725, when the dictatorship of Beau Nash had made Bath famous throughout the length and breadth of the land, Oliver took up his residence there and soon became the most eminent physician in this Queen of Watering-Places. His *Practical Essay on the Use and Abuse of warm Bathing in Gouty Cases*, published in 1751, became a classic work on the subject and ran into three editions before his death. The Bath Oliver biscuit, for which alone his name will be remembered, was invented by him shortly before his death. The recipe was entrusted to his coachman Atkins, who subsequently opened a shop in Green Street and acquired a large fortune through the sale of the celebrated biscuit.

Quite apart, however, from these achievements, Oliver stands out in the history of Bath as a man of intense practical charity who, while achieving fame, never forgot the plight of those who were less fortunate than himself. His compassion for others found expression in the foundation of the Bath General Hospital —now called the Royal Mineral Water Hospital—for poor persons who needed the healing waters but could not afford the luxury of being invalids. In this noble work, which stands to this day as an ever-present reminder of his zeal for the poor and the sick, Oliver was zealously assisted by Beau Nash, Ralph Allen, and the elder Wood—the four great luminaries in the Bath firmament at this period. Oliver himself was appointed physician to the Hospital in 1740 and his close friend and collaborator Jerry Pierce became the surgeon. The two were painted together by William Hoare in the act of interviewing the patients who clamoured for admission to this beneficent institution. In his person and life's work William Oliver represents all that was best in the gay and frivolous age of Beau Nash. Behind the brilliant and glittering social façade, the dances and balls and assemblies, there went on all the time that slow and steady work of healing and amelioration which had drawn the Romans of old to the waters of Bath.

It is fitting that we should have first mentioned the name of Ralph Allen in connection with a work of charity, for his whole life was one of service to others. As M. Barbeau so truly observes,

"In the frivolous Bath of Beau Nash he represents the solid qualities and the virtues of private life. He is also the great civic figure; it is he who presides over the material development of the city of his adoption, encourages architecture in the person of Wood, whose talent he discovered, and, seconding the architect's vast plans and those of his son, assists in the amazing transformation of Bath." Like Dr. Oliver, Ralph Allen was a Cornishman, but of very humble origin. His father was a small innkeeper. At the age of eighteen he entered the post-office at Bath and, so the story goes, first proved his mettle by discovering a Jacobite plot which he promptly denounced to Marshal Wade. The Marshal expressed his gratitude by securing his appointment as postmaster of Bath and by marrying him to his natural daughter. From this hour Allen never looked back. Gifted with exceptional resources of ingenuity and enterprise, he instituted radical reforms in the postal service which make him stand with Palmer (another Bath man) and Rowland Hill as one of the founders of the modern postal system. Not content with these triumphs, Ralph Allen invented ingenious devices for exploiting the rich stone-quarries at Combe Down, near Bath. His enterprise made it possible for Bath stone to be conveyed from the top of Combe Down to the River Avon, where it was shipped to Bristol, London, and all the major ports of England. In this way Bath freestone rapidly acquired a national celebrity and Allen may thus be accounted as largely responsible for the use of this superb medium by the Woods in their rebuilding and prodigious enlargement of Bath.

If Allen had achieved no more than this—the reform of the postal service and the exploitation of the Bath quarries—his name would be an honoured one in the history both of his city and country. As it is, his chief claim on the gratitude of posterity rests in his discriminate patronage of a brilliant group of men who foregathered at his beautiful house, Prior Park. Here it was that the leading figures of the kingdom in art, literature, and politics enjoyed the hospitality of one who never obtruded himself but was dearly loved by all. To give any adequate knowledge of the range of acquaintance of this eighteenth-century Mæcenas would be to mention most of the famous names of that illustrious age. Only one or two indications can be given. Alexander Pope,

28 Prior Park on its completion, *ca.* 1750, showing Ralph Allen's Tramway for carrying up Bath Stone from the Quarries

29   Prior Park: the Garden Front and Terrace, built by John Wood the Elder

who was never a very easy companion, became a bosom friend of
Allen, who made his acquaintance by inviting him to stay
at Prior Park after reading and greatly admiring the first volume
of his letters. From 1736 to 1743 Pope was regularly at Prior
Park, often for long periods at a time. It was he who, with his
host's willing concurrence, invited Dr. Warburton to Prior Park
and thus established a friendship which led to Warburton's
rapid advancement in the world of affairs. Pope and Warburton
planned together the contents of the last book of the *Dunciad*
in Allen's library at Prior Park. Here the great actor Garrick
met his old rival Quin, and Gainsborough was a frequent visitor.
William Pitt, Earl of Chatham, the Great Commoner, who
was member of parliament for Bath during the years 1757–66,
mainly as a result of Allen's influence, loved the society of Prior
Park and, on Allen's death in 1764, wrote this glowing tribute
to his widow: "I will only say that, in Mr. Allen, mankind has
lost such a benevolent and tender friend as, I fear, not all the
example of his virtues will have power to raise up to the world
again. Admiring his life and regretting the shortness of it, I
shall ever respectfully cherish his memory, and rank the con-
tinuation of the favourable opinion and friendship of a truly
good man amongst the happiest advantages and the first honours
which fortune may have bestowed upon my life." This is indeed
an impressive testimony from a man so little given to fulsome
eulogy as the Earl of Chatham. But the last word on Ralph
Allen may fairly be given to Henry Fielding, who was very often
at Prior Park and has portrayed his host at full length under the
guise of Squire Allworthy in *Tom Jones*:

"Neither Mr. Allworthy's house nor his heart were shut against
any part of mankind; but they were both more particularly
open to men of merit. To say the truth, this was the only house
in the kingdom where you were sure to gain a dinner by deserving
it.

"Above all others, men of genius and learning shared the
principal place in his favour; and in these he had much discern-
ment; for though he had missed the advantage of a learned
education, yet, being blessed with vast natural abilities, he had
so well profited by a vigorous, though late application to letters,
and by much conversation with men of eminence in this way,

that he was himself a very competent judge in most kinds of literature.

"It is no wonder that, in an age when this kind of merit is so little in fashion and so slenderly provided for, persons possessed of it should very eagerly flock to a place where they were sure of being received with great complaisance, indeed, where they might employ almost the same advantages of a liberal fortune as if they were entitled to it in their own right; for Mr. Allworthy was not one of those generous persons who are ready most bountifully to bestow meat, drink, and lodging on men of wit and learning, for which they expect no other return but entertainment, instruction, and subserviency; in a word, that such persons should be enrolled in the number of domestics, without wearing their master's clothes or receiving wages.

"On the contrary, every person in this house was perfect master of his own time; and as he might at his pleasure satisfy all his appetites within the restrictions only of law, virtue and religion: so he might, if his health required, or his inclination prompted him to temperance, or even to abstinence, absent himself from any meals or retire from them whenever he was so disposed, without even a solicitation to the contrary: for, indeed, such solicitations from superiors always savour very strongly of commands. But all here were free from impertinence, not only those whose company is in all other places esteemed a favour from their equality of fortune, but even those whose indigent circumstances made such an eleemosynary abode convenient to them, and who are therefore less welcome to a great man's table because they stand in need of it."

With this moving and sincere tribute we may fittingly conclude our account of one who, as long as art and culture are honoured among men, will be regarded as a modern Mæcenas of a singularly lovable character.

Nash: Oliver: Allen. All contributed in their degree to the fame of eighteenth-century Bath. But the picture would be incomplete without the John Woods, father and son, whose architectural genius transformed the city from a small provincial watering-place into a second Pompeii. The classical austerity, elegance, and dignity of eighteenth-century Bath has won renown among all persons of fine sensibility and good taste.

How did this miracle come to pass? How could the genius of classical antiquity flower again in Georgian England?

As we have seen, a peculiar conjunction of circumstances prompted the creation of the Bath of the eighteenth century. It was, *par excellence,* the summer colony of the *beau monde*: the resort of the leaders of fashion, wit, and public affairs. Everything demanded that in its architectural display Bath should become a "show-place", the expression of the best taste of the ruling class. And as classicism was in the ascendant throughout this period, it was imperative that the city should display the strictest classical proportions and a most exact and painstaking fidelity to the example of Greece and Rome.

When Beau Nash became King of Bath at the beginning of the century the influence of Inigo Jones and Christopher Wren had made itself felt throughout the length and breadth of the kingdom. Gothic style was everywhere attacked and abused. The classical world was the all-sufficient model: the very touchstone of good taste. The first quarter of the eighteenth century in Bath, therefore, "seems to form a link between the old Tudor building—with its gables, small mullioned windows (of which examples remain at the back of Broad Street and Westgate Street), narrow courses, low ceilings, and irregular planning—and the new Palladian manner with its ample interiors, exact proportions, and ornate façades". Not much of this early work —the pre-Wood architecture, as we may call it—has survived. The Pump Room, built in 1706, was replaced by the present more spacious building at the end of the century. Harrison's Assembly Rooms ("The Lower Rooms") were erected in 1708 against the outside of the city wall on the south side and were demolished in the nineteenth century. The houses in Orange Grove are mostly of a later period, though first planned in the pre-Wood era. There are, however, houses in Trim Street, Lilliput Alley, and Saw Close (above all, Beau Nash's house, which is now the Sedan-Chair Café) which were planned and built in the first quarter of the century on the strictest classical model. But the greater glories of Bath all belong to the age of the Woods.

John Wood the elder was born in Yorkshire in the year 1704. Spending his early manhood in his native county as a surveyor of roads, he settled at Bath in 1727 at the behest of Ralph Allen, whose fertile mind was fully alive to the great potentialities of Bath freestone as a building material. This magnificent oolite limestone, the colour of rich honey and singularly responsive to the mellowing effects of rain and storm, is a great incentive to an aspiring architect. "I procured a plan of the town", Wood tells us in his *Description of Bath*, "which was sent me in Yorkshire in the summer of the year 1725, where I, at my leisure hours, formed one design for the ground at the north-west corner of the city, and another for the land on the north-east side of the town and river." John Wood was an ardent disciple of that school of classical architecture which is known in England as Palladian. That is to say, his master was Vitruvius as understood by the men of the Italian Renaissance. With the constant assistance of Ralph Allen and the blessing of Beau Nash, he set about the task of covering the valley and hills of Bath with noble and elegant houses expressive of the true spirit of classical antiquity.

John Wood's first achievement in Bath was to complete the rebuilding of the Hospital of St. John the Baptist in the vicinity of the Cross Bath. Its simple dignity and good proportions are a clear harbinger of what was to be expected from his fertile genius. His next work of importance was Chandos Buildings, the large house on the south of which was rebuilt in 1727 for the Duke of Chandos. The houses constitute a large three-sided court which Wood essayed in vain to turn into a square, never being able to purchase the property. Then, with the building of Queen Square during the years 1728–35, Wood came into his own as one of the foremost architects in the kingdom. I find it hard to bestow sufficient praise on this perfect specimen of classical architecture. I can only say that, with the possible exception of Prior Park, I have always regarded it as the finest achievement of the Woods. Less spectacular than the Circus, incomparably less impressive than the Crescent, Queen Square surpasses both in its exquisite proportions and its uncompromising classic severity. Look at the grand façade on the north side of the square. There, with the Corinthian colonnade, the elegant sash-windows, and noble architrave, you see the true consummation of English Palladian architecture. The ancient world has been granted a second

30 Sham Castle: Ralph Allen's Folly near Bath

31 The Palladian Bridge, Prior Park

33   General Wolfe's House

32   Ralph Allen's Town House

spring at the magic hand of a builder of genius. When complete, the Square consisted of 25 houses, if we omit the Lodge in the centre of the west side. During the greater part of the eighteenth century it was one of the most fashionable places of residence in Bath. But then, with new crescents and terraces springing up on the hills and Bathwick suddenly being transformed into a fashionable suburb of Bath, Queen Square ceased for a time to be the chosen resort of the *beau monde*.

Gay Street, which leads from Queen Square to the Circus and was named after its ground landlord Robert Gay, was built some twenty years after the completion of the masterpiece we have just been considering. It is in the same tradition, consisting mostly of small houses, some of which are richly ornamented with Corinthian pilasters and other classical *motifs*. At the top of this steep ascent—for Gay Street is essentially an artery linking two major works—is (I quote Miss Sitwell), "the superb Circus, with its fantastic and magnificent houses of the Ionic, Doric, and Corinthian styles". This *pièce de résistance* was planned by the elder Wood and put into execution by his son. It was finished in 1765. "It is very evident", says Mowbray Green, our leading authority on the eighteenth-century architecture of Bath, "that in elaborating the Circus with its three distinct orders—Doric, Ionic, and Corinthian—and its wonderful array of coupled columns, three hundred and twenty-four pairs in all, with the bands of ornament at the upper and lower storeys, and the acorns crowning each coupled order, Wood intended to impress the spectator from a near point of view, knowing well that in such a form as a circle a distant view would be impossible." Personally, I find the Circus somewhat oppressive. It is too openly conscious of its virtuosity, too obviously intended to impress and amaze. I would never leave a house in Queen Square to occupy the most magnificent dwelling that the Circus can offer. Tobias Smollett seems to have had strong views on this point. He makes that irascible and chronic invalid Matthew Bramble declare that "the Circus is a pretty bauble, contrived for show, and looks like Vespasian's amphitheatre turned outside in". There could surely be no more devastating comment.

On leaving the Circus, one passes down the quiet and secluded Brock Street to reach the spacious eminence of the Royal Cres-

cent. Although this carries us a few years beyond the age of
Beau Nash—the Crescent was not begun until 1767 and was
finished some eight years later—the whole conception and plan
of this dazzling achievement is eloquent of the halcyon days of
Bath. It is the work of the younger Wood, the worthy son of
worthy sire. Its grace and dignity are unsurpassed anywhere in
England. With fields in which sheep and cattle graze stretching
before it and with a superb view of the city and Beechen Cliff
beyond, the Crescent is the most arresting spectacle that Bath
can offer. Yet its architectural plan is simplicity itself. A basement storey of unrelieved plainness supports a large Ionic
order, the columns of which rise through two storeys and are
crowned by an entablature. The parapet is a plain open balustrade. "The effect is obtained by the dominating order and the
bold sweeping circular lines over, unbroken to the roof." In
these three pieces, Queen Square, the Circus, the Royal Crescent,
so different in detail and yet in feeling all belonging to the great
abiding tradition of classical architecture, a natural climax is
reached in the transformation of Bath. The wandering spirit of
Vitruvius and Palladius has found a lasting refuge in the Queen
City of the West.

An easy morning's walk will take one from the heart of Bath
to Prior Park, the beautiful home of Ralph Allen, which was
designed and built by the elder Wood during the years 1735-43.
It lies near the head of the lovely combe that stretches from the
bottom of Widcombe Hill to Combe Down. As the name implies,
this was once the property of Bath cathedral priory and it
belongs to-day to the Christian Brothers who maintain the
Catholic tradition of the place. This magnificent mansion, which
is truly consonant to the generous spirit of Robert Allen,
is the cynosure of the surrounding countryside. Like the Royal
Crescent, it owes much of its dignity and charm to its lofty
situation, standing well above the ancient city and its environs.
"The scheme of the design", writes Mowbray Green, "was three-
fold—a central mansion with east and west wings and a pavilion
placed between the more important buildings and joined up to
them by a colonnade. In the execution of the work, however,
the wing of offices was joined up to the pavilion and thus brought
nearer to the house on the east side, while on the west they remain

34, 35   The Circus, built by the Woods

36   Plaster Decoration by the Franchinis in 15, Queen Square, the house of John Wood the Elder

detached." A massive Corinthian colonnade on the north front
arrests the eye from afar and gives the *coup de grâce* to this
exquisite specimen of Palladian architecture. Below the terraces
and gardens at the foot of the slope on the north side is the
Palladian Bridge which is almost an identical copy of that built
by Robert Morris at Wilton House in 1736. It spans part of the
old fish-ponds which belonged to the monks of Bath. Strongly
Venetian in character and inspiration, this wonderful bridge,
the crowning glory of Prior Park, was built sometime between
the years 1750 and 1760.

Now return to the centre of the city of Bath to consider some
other architectural achievements of the age of the Woods and
Beau Nash. The Royal Mineral Water Hospital, close to the
old city walls, invites special attention. This charitable
foundation was, as we have seen, the product of the joint
exertions of the four founders of modern Bath: Beau Nash,
Dr. Oliver, Ralph Allen, and the elder Wood. Its imposing
façade and fine proportions reveal the high talent of the elder
Wood, who began work on this building in 1738. The foundation-
stone was laid with great ceremony by Sir William Pulteney,
who later became Earl of Bath.

In his original building-plans John Wood had made provision
for a Grand Parade on the south side of Queen Square. This,
however, was never realized and Wood was persuaded to transfer
his attention to the south-east corner of the city which sloped
down to the river and was little better than a bog at the beginning of the eighteenth century. The orchard of the monks was
situated here in medieval times. In July 1739 Wood signed his
contract for the land where the North and South Parades now
stand and spent the rest of the year in draining the site. The
whole of the North or Grand Parade, including Duke Street and
Pierrepont Street, was not completed until soon after 1748.
There is a plain unadorned simplicity about the whole work
which is in the most austere tradition of the eighteenth century.
The South Parade is slightly different in its plan. There is a
double break at the centre and a balustrade crowns the plain
façade of the houses.

Finally, from the abundance of fine domestic architecture
associated with the age of Beau Nash, one may single out the

group of buildings in the west of the city inspired by the architect
John Strahan. This almost forgotten architect, whom his
jealous rival John Wood hardly condescends to mention in his
Description of Bath, came to Bristol about the year 1726 to
practice as a land-surveyor and builder. He soon came to enjoy
the patronage of John Hobbs, a Bristol merchant, who com-
missioned him to build on a large area of ground outside the
West Gate. So during the years 1727–36 there came into being
Kingsmead Square, Avon Street, Monmouth Street, and Beaufort
Square. Although situated in a relatively unfashionable quarter
of the city, these plain unpretentious buildings have a quiet
charm which is all their own. No one will deny that John
Strahan had thoroughly mastered the great and guiding principles of classical architecture. The Quay, now called the Broad
Quay, is also the work of Strahan and was built at about the
same time.

The completion of the Royal Crescent in 1775 marks the
glorious end of that efflorescence of classical architecture in
Bath which began with the advent of Beau Nash at the beginning
of the century. Other achievements were to follow in the purest
classical vein, but after the Crescent they must always appear
as something of an anti-climax. Three-quarters of a century
may seem a short time in the history of an ancient city. Yet in
this brief period, the lifetime of one man, Bath was utterly
transformed from a not very distinguished provincial town into
a Mecca of noble Palladian architecture.

37   St. James's Square: from a plate by A. Woodroffe (*ca.* 1820)

38   Queen Square, built by John Wood the Elder:
from a plate by W. Watts (1819)

39   Ralph Allen: from the portrait by William Hoare in
     the Pump Room

40   Sheridan as Pizzaro : a caricature by Gillray of 1799

5

The Bath of Smollett and Sheridan

THE DEATH OF BEAU NASH IN 1761, WHICH HAD BEEN SHORTLY preceded by that of the elder Wood and was quickly followed by that of Ralph Allen and Dr. Oliver, symbolized the end of an epoch in the history of Bath. The privileged aristocratic society created and nurtured by Nash in the heyday of his influence had already undergone great changes before his death in extreme old age. Bath was beginning to confront its nemesis. Made popular and fashionable by the organizing genius of the Beau, its very popularity was the primary cause of its gradual decline. For when Bath was invaded by the mob, it ceased to attract its aristocratic *clientèle* and to be the chosen resort of Polite Society. Nash has no successor of comparable calibre as Master of the Ceremonies. A tone of mediocrity began to invade the city. And this spelt the beginning of the end.

Nevertheless Bath had a long Indian summer in the second half of the eighteenth century and was frequented by several eminent men of letters that sang its praises in prose and verse. It also attracted a large number of minor poets who are known collectively as the Water Poets, as their common theme was the manifold allurements of a fashionable watering-place. Easily the best-known and most skilful of these Water Poets was Christopher Anstey, a scholar of Eton and King's, Cambridge, of which College he was elected a Fellow in 1745. The fact that Anstey had taken Holy Orders in the Anglican Church did not deter him from writing in 1766 a poem called *The New Bath Guide* which for scurrility and wit yields to none of the productions of that broad-minded age. That severe critic, Horace Walpole, greeted this work with something like rhapsody in a letter to his friend George Montagu:

"What pleasure have you to come! There is a new thing published called the *New Bath Guide*. It stole into the world, and for a fortnight no soul looked into it, concluding its name was its true name. No such thing. It is a set of letters in verses, in all kinds of verses, describing the life of Bath, and, incidentally, everything else; but so much wit; so much humour, fun and poetry, so much originality never met together before. Then the man has a better ear than Dryden or Handel. *A propos* to Dryden he has burlesqued his St. Cecilia, that you will never read it again without laughing. There is a description of a milliner's box in all the terms of landscape, painted lawns and chequered shades, and a Moravian ode, and a Methodist ditty, that are incomparable and the best names that were ever composed. I can say it by heart, though a quarto, and if I had time would write it you down, for it is not yet reprinted, and not one to be had."

Miss Edith Sitwell emphatically dissociates herself from this glowing verdict and views Anstey as little better than a second-rate poetaster. This, I think, is rather harsh. Though never a great poet and totally lacking the felicity of an Alexander Pope in the turn of his couplets, Christopher Anstey displays a genuine ability and wit. He gives us a diverting picture of that Bath society which had ceased to be the preserve of a fashionable *élite* and was now being invaded by a motley crowd of persons of all classes.

Anstey's poem takes the form of letters from a typical family who visited Bath during the Season. This consisted of Simkin Blunderhead, his sister Prudence, their cousin Jenny, and a maid Tabitha Runt. The protocol was strictly observed on their arrival in Bath:

"No City, dear Mother, this City excels
For charming sweet Sounds both of Fiddles and Bells;
I thought, like a Fool, that they only would ring
For a wedding, or Judge, or the Birth of a King;
But I found 'twas for Me that the good-natur'd People
Rung so hard that I thought they would pull down the Steeple,
So I took out my Purse as I hate to be shabby,
And paid all the Men when they came from the Abbey."

Next day this family, which found lodgings at the Bear Inn, received a visit from a Bath doctor:

"He determin'd our Cases at length (G-d preserve us).
I'm Bilious, I find, and the Women are Nervous;
Their Systems relax'd, and all turn'd topsy-turvy,
With Hypochondriacs, Obstructions, and Scurvy;

And these are Distempers He must know the whole on,
For He talk'd of the Peritoneum and Colon,
Of Phlegmatic Humours oppressing the Women,
From fœculent Matter that swells the Abdomen;
But the Noise I have heard in my Bowels like Thunder
Is a Flatus, I find, in my left Hypochonder."

So the Blunderhead family took the waters and played their full part in the gaieties and pleasures of the city. Anstey uses the occasion for directing the shafts of his wit at the Methodists who were represented at Bath by that most unlovable woman, Selina, Countess of Huntingdon. This distinguished convert had attracted around her at Bath a fashionable circle whom she prevailed upon to listen to the sermons of her chaplain, Mr. Whitefield. These addresses breathed the spirit of the purest Calvinism. The Countess herself was on the directing council of the Methodists and was officially dubbed "a mother in Israel". She attracted both of the Wesleys to Bath as well as Mr. Whitefield. Charles Wesley went so far as to say that in visiting Bath he was "attacking Satan at his headquarters"! The Countess of Huntingdon, firmly persuaded of her own salvation and that of her well-to-do followers, was a spiritual snob of the first order. The narrow and restricting influence of her sect was often accompanied by something that looked very like hypocrisy. This it was that Anstey saw fit to pillory in a merciless manner in the letter of Prudence Blunderhead to Lady Elizabeth Modeless.

" Hearken, Lady Betty, hearken,
To the dismal News I tell;
How your Friends are all embarking,
For the fiery Gulph of Hell.

Brother Simkin's grown a Rakehell,
Cards and dances ev'ry Day.
Jenny laughs at Tabernacle,
Tabby Runt is gone astray.

Blessed I, tho' once rejected,
Like a little wand'ring Sheep;
Who this Morning was elected,
By a Vision in my Sleep:

For I dream'd an Apparition
Came, like ROGER, from Above;
Saying, by Divine Commission
I must fill you full of Love.

Just with ROGER's Head of Hair on.
ROGER's Mouth, and pious Smile;
Sweet, methinks, as Beard of AARON
Dropping down with holy Oil.

I began to fall a kicking,
Panted, struggl'd, strove in vain;
When the Spirit whipt so quick in,
I was cur'd of all my Pain.

First I thought it was the Night-Mare
Lay so heavy on my Breast;
But I found new Joy and Light there,
When with Heav'nly Love possesst.

Come again then, Apparition,
Finish what thou hast begun;
ROGER, stay, Thou Soul's Physician,
I with thee my Race will run.

Faith her Chariot has appointed.
Now we're stretching for the Goal;
All the Wheels with Grace anointed,
Up to Heav'n to drive my Soul."

Roger, one hardly need add, was a Methodist preacher who was staying at "The Bear" and had conceived a marked affection for Prudence Blunderhead!

The general impression of Bath society in the later eighteenth century that emerges from the study of Anstey's satire is amply confirmed by the three great novels of Tobias Smollett. Smollett was a frequent visitor to Bath throughout his life and resided there for long periods at a time. A doctor by profession, if not by inclination, he wrote in 1752 an *Essay on the External Use of Water, with particular Remarks on the Mineral Waters of Bath.* But his name will ever be associated with Bath on account of those novels in which he portrayed the seamy side of the life of this great watering-place with merciless severity. In *Roderick Random* (1749) and *Peregrine Pickle* (1751) we are introduced

42, 43   Bath Rococo

41   The Staircase of 15, Queen Square
(now removed)

44 The Doorway of General Wolfe's House in Trim Street

45 The Doorway of 14, Alfred Street, with its wrought iron torch-extinguishers

46 A Regency Fanlight

to the motley crew of rogues, charlatans, mountebanks, and strumpets who lay behind the gay and glittering façade of the Queen of the West. The adventures of these persons illustrate all the vices, intrigues, and corruptions of a society which valued pleasure and luxury and nothing else. Together, these two novels constitute something like a Plain Man's Guide to Eighteenth-Century Wickedness. The reader who wishes to excavate this cesspool cannot do better than peruse and annotate both works. Even if disedified, he cannot fail to be amused.

The tone of *Humphrey Clinker*, Smollett's most mature work, written in 1771, the year of his death, is somewhat different. This misanthropic Scotsman, who looked upon all Englishmen as leagued in perpetual conspiracy against North Britons, acquired some balance and serenity only in the last years of his life. A kinder, more humane, more sympathetic note is to be found in this, his last and greatest work. The portraiture of life at Bath is exceptionally vivid and obviously owes much to Christopher Anstey's *New Bath Guide*, published some five years previously. We are introduced to a family, Matthew Bramble, his sister Tabitha Bramble (a plain reminiscence of Anstey's Tabitha Runt), and their niece and nephew, Lydia and Jerry Melford, who visit Bath in search of a cure for Matthew Bramble's chronic ill-health. This irascible but not unlovable valetudinarian and his family found lodgings on the South Parade, a situation chosen "for its being near the Bath, and remote from the noise of carriages". Very soon afterwards "the town-waits, in the passage below, struck up their music" and the family went through the usual elaborate ritual of Bath society. Smollett puts in the mouth of Matthew Bramble—for it is an epistolary novel— words which show clearly how the popularity of Bath had proved in truth to be its nemesis:

"Every upstart of fortune, harnessed in the trappings of the mode, presents himself at Bath, as in the very focus of observation. Clerks and factors from the East Indies, loaded with the spoil of plundered provinces; planters, negro drivers, and hucksters, from our American plantations, enriched they know not how; agents, commissaries, and contractors, who have fattened, in two successive wars, on the blood of the nation; usurers, brokers, and jobbers of every kind; men of low birth,

and no breeding, have found themselves suddenly translated into
a state of affluence, unknown to former ages; and no wonder
that their brains should be intoxicated with pride, vanity, and
presumption. Knowing no other criterion of greatness, but the
ostentation of wealth, they discharge their affluence without
taste or conduct, through every channel of the most absurd
extravagance; and all of them hurry to Bath, because here,
without any further qualification, they can mingle with the
princes and nobles of the land. Even the wives and daughters
of low tradesmen, who, like shovel-nosed sharks, prey upon
the blubber of those uncouth whales of fortune, are infected with
the same rage of displaying their importance; and the slightest
indisposition serves them for a pretext to insist upon being
conveyed to Bath, where they may hobble country-dances and
cotillons among lordlings, 'squires, counsellors, and clergy.
These delicate creatures from Bedfordbury, Butcher-row,
Crutched-Friers, and Botolph-lane cannot breathe in the gross
air of the Lower Town, or conform to the vulgar rules of a
common lodging-house; the husband, therefore, must provide
an entire house, or elegant apartments in the new buildings.
Such is the composition of what is called the fashionable company at Bath; where a very inconsiderable proportion of genteel
people are lost in a mob of impudent plebeians, who have
neither understanding nor judgment, nor the least idea of
propriety and decorum; and seem to enjoy nothing so much as
an opportunity of insulting their betters."

There is the authentic picture of the Bath that followed
hard upon the death of Beau Nash and Ralph Allen: a busy
jostling crowd of high-born and low-born all engaged in a frantic
round of pleasure and diversion, an easy prey to sharks and
fortune-hunters.

The successful "gate-crashing" of the *plebs* into the exclusive
pleasures of noblemen and gentlemen is also commented upon
by Jerry Melford in one of his letters to his learned friend at
Oxford:

"I was extremely diverted, last ball-night, to see the Master
of the Ceremonies leading, with great solemnity, to the upper-end
of the room, an antiquated Abigail, dressed in her lady's best
clothes; whom he (I suppose) mistook for some countess just

arrived at the Bath. The ball was opened by a Scotch lord, with a mulatto heiress from St. Christopher's; and the gay Colonel Tinsel danced all the evening with the daughter of an eminent tinman from the borough of Southwark. Yesterday morning, at the Pump-room, I saw a broken-winded Wapping landlady squeeze through a circle of peers, to salute her brandy merchant, who stood by the window, prop'd upon crutches; and a paralytic attorney of Shoe-lane, in shuffling up to the bar, kicked the shins of the Chancellor of England, while his lordship, in a cut bob, drank a glass of water at the pump."

Smollett, whose vivid and outspoken portraiture of distinctive human types is one of his greatest merits as a novelist, has a brilliant thumbnail sketch of a moneyed fool who "cut a dash" in Bath society at this period:

"Jack Holder, who was intended for a parson, has succeeded to an estate of two thousand a year, by the death of his elder brother. He is now at the Bath, driving about in a phaeton and four, with French-horns. He has treated with turtle and claret at all the taverns in Bath and Bristol, till his guests are gorged with good cheer: he has bought a dozen suits of fine clothes, by the advice of the Master of the Ceremonies, under whose tuition he has entered himself: he has lost some hundreds at billiards to sharpers, and taken one of the nymphs of Avon-street into keeping; but, finding all these channels insufficient to drain him of his current cash, his counsellor has engaged him to give a general tea-drinking to-morrow at Wiltshire's room."

Jack Holder must have been a rather common type in the Bath which Tobias Smollett knew so well. The "nymphs of Avon-street" figure very largely in the popular literature, the ballads and broadsheets, of the time. Creatures less ethereal than these it would be hard to encounter!

Before we say farewell to Smollett, it would be well to see the impressions of Bath that he places in the mouth of Lydia Melford, the young and attractive niece of Matthew Bramble:

"Bath is to me a new world. All is gaiety, good-humour, and diversion. The eye is continually entertained with the splendour of dress and equipage; and the ear with the sound of coaches, chaises, chairs, and other carriages. The merry bells ring round, from morn till night. Then we are welcomed by the city-waits

in our own lodgings: we have music in the Pump-room every
morning, cotillons every fore-noon in the rooms, balls twice a
week, and concerts every other night, besides private assemblies
and parties without number. . . . The Square, the Circus, and the
Parades, put you in mind of the sumptuous palaces represented
in prints and pictures; and the new buildings, such as Princes-
row, Harlequin's-row, Bladud's-row, and twenty other rows,
look like so many enchanted castles, raised on hanging terraces.
At eight in the morning, we go in déshabillé to the Pump-room,
which is crowded like a Welsh fair; and there you see the
highest quality, and the lowest trades-folks, jostling each other,
without ceremony, hail-fellow-well-met. . . . Hard by the Pump-
room is a coffee-house for the ladies; but my aunt says, young
girls are not admitted, inasmuch as the conversation turns upon
politics, scandal, philosophy, and other subjects above our
capacity; but we are allowed to accompany them to the booksellers' shops, which are charming places of resort; where we
read novels, plays, pamphlets, and newspapers, for so small a
subscription as a crown a quarter; and in these offices of intelligence (as my brother calls them), all the reports of the day, and
all the private transactions of the Bath, are first entered and
discussed. From the bookseller's shop, we make a tour through
the milliners and toy-men; and commonly stop at Mr. Gill's,
the pastry-cook, to take a jelly, a tart, or a small bason of
vermicelli. There is, moreover, another place of entertainment on
the other side of the water, opposite to the Grove; to which the
company cross over in a boat. It is called Spring Gardens; a
sweet retreat, laid out in walks and ponds, and parterres of
flowers; and there is a long-room for breakfasting and dancing.
. . . They say, dancing at Spring Gardens, where the air is moist,
is recommended to them as an excellent cure for the rheumatism.
I have been twice at the play; where, notwithstanding the
excellence of the performers, the gaiety of the company, and the
decorations of the theatre, which are very fine, I could not help
reflecting, with a sigh, upon our poor homely representations
at Gloucester."

Perhaps the most interesting thing in this vivid account is the
reference to the "private assemblies and parties without number"
which had become such a distinctive feature of the life of the

city. These private gatherings had been absolutely forbidden under the dictatorship of Beau Nash. The Beau had made it his deliberate policy to gather up all the strands of social life into the public and official gatherings at the Pump Room and Assembly Rooms. Once the principle of private parties was admitted, the whole social structure of Bath was shaken to its very foundations.

While Smollett was writing his great swan-song *Humphrey Clinker*, a meteor crossed the Bath stage in the person of Richard Brinsley Sheridan. This is not the place to recount the brilliant career of this exceptional individual as dramatist and parliamentary orator, for that is now part of the general history of the country. Suffice it to say that whatever Sheridan turned his hand to, he imprinted with his own indelible mark. Whether as dramatist, orator, parliamentarian, conversationalist, or social lion, Sheridan shone with a peculiar brilliance. The intimate friend of the Prince of Wales, the confidant of Fox, the colleague of Burke, his abilities were as phenomenal as his social accomplishments. His association with Bath belongs to his early days. His father Thomas Sheridan, an Irishman who won a living as an actor and an elocutionist, settled in Bath in 1770 with his wife and four children. Mrs. Sheridan was a woman of some literary ability who had produced eight years previously a play called *A Journey to Bath*, in which the characters of the place were gently satirized. It is clear that the great dramatist owed much of his exceptional talent to his mother, which he implicitly acknowledged when he borrowed one of her characters, Mrs. Tryfort, as the prototype of Mrs. Malaprop.

Before he had written his first play, *The Rivals*, Sheridan had won something like national fame by his romantic elopement with the beautiful Elizabeth Ann Linley. This is one of the classic love-affairs of the eighteenth century. Miss Linley was one of a very gifted family, all of whom excelled in the world of music. Thomas Linley, her father, taught music and singing at Bath and was considered to be without a serious rival in his profession. Elizabeth Ann herself took part in her father's concerts and oratorios from a tender age, enrapturing audiences at Bath, Oxford, and London with the beauty of her voice and form. "Miss Linley's beauty", Horace Walpole observed, "is in the superlative degree. The King admires her and ogles her as much as he dares to do in so holy a place as an oratorio." (High praise indeed, for Farmer George was not lightly weaned from the path of impeccable rectitude!) Her intelligence, her wit, and her modesty and grace of manner equalled the astonishing beauty of her features and her divine voice. It was only to be expected that suitors clamoured for the favours and attentions of Miss Linley. Charles Sheridan, Richard's elder brother, was one of her first admirers; another was Halhed, an Oxford undergraduate. And there were many more. But Thomas Linley had definite plans for his beautiful and gifted daughter. He wished her to marry a certain Mr. Long, a Wiltshire landowner who was sixty years of age but very rich. The marriage was fully arranged. The jewels were given. The settlement was drawn up. But, we are told, "talk raged in the city, and public opinion blamed the greedy parents as much as the sexagenarian lover". The general disapproval at the bartering-away of this lovely woman was expressed by Foote, the actor and author, who in a play called *The Maid of Bath* portrayed a beautiful Miss Linnet forced into marrying "an old fusty, shabby, shuffling, money-loving, water-drinking, milk-marring, amorous old hunk, Mr. Solomon Flint."

Meanwhile the victim herself was asserting her independence of her father's wishes. She wrote secretly to Mr. Long, begging him to desist in his attentions as she secretly loved another. Mr. Long behaved very handsomely, complied with her wishes, and when her father threatened him with a lawsuit, settled £3000 on Elizabeth Ann of his own accord. A far more dangerous man now stepped in, one Major Matthews who, though married, led a life of great dissipation and knew no scruple. He proceeded "to harass the young girl with secret and objectionable attentions, soon followed by disgraceful proposals." This threw her into the arms of Sheridan, who first appeared to her as a disinterested friend, only concerned to save her from the dreadful Matthews. Together they planned to seek refuge on the Continent and a French convent was regarded as the best asylum. A female companion was to go with them as a pledge of the good faith of both parties. So one evening, when her father and sister were absent at a concert, Elizabeth left the Royal Crescent in a

47   Taking the Waters

48   A Visit from the Doctor

From Rowlandson's "Comforts of Bath" (1798)

49   A Ball in the Assembly Rooms

50   Invalids' Diet

From Rowlandson's "Comforts of Bath" (1798)

51   Drinking the Waters

52   A Spill on the Slopes

From Rowlandson's "Comforts of Bath" (1798)

53   Milsom Street: from the plate by J. C. Nattes (1806)

sedan-chair sent her by Sheridan and entered a post-chaise in which the female companion was waiting. The three quickly travelled to London and set sail for Dunkirk. It was only then that Sheridan declared his love to Miss Linley, urging her to marry him without delay. As she "already preferred Sheridan to every other man" she willingly consented, and the two were married in a village near Calais by a priest "accustomed to such unions". Shortly afterwards, when explanations had been offered to Elizabeth's father, the married couple returned to Bath.

It was now that the thwarted Major Matthews showed his fire. He wrote a series of savage letters to Sheridan, full of threats and insults. These had the desired effect. Angry and proud, Sheridan drove with seconds to Matthews' house in London and a duel took place in a tavern. This ended in a victory for Sheridan, as Matthews was worsted and wrote a note apologizing for his conduct. But the incorrigible Major retired to Wales only to brew more trouble. His friends persuaded him to challenge Sheridan to another duel. This he did, and the two adversaries met again at Kingsdown, a hill near Bath. In this second duel Matthews got the better of his rival and Sheridan was taken to a neighbouring inn in a very bad way. Miss Linley (as she was still officially known, for the marriage was clandestine) rushed to her husband's bedside, nursed him to health, and, finally, married him officially and publicly in London in July 1773. Matthews never dared to show his face again in Bath.

Some writers have delighted to compare the theme of *The Rivals*, which was first produced at Covent Garden in January 1775, with Sheridan's own romance, and to regard it as in part a chapter in autobiography. This view is extremely superficial, for, despite external resemblances such as rivals, duels, and the *mise en scène*, there is no character in the play remotely resembling either Sheridan or Matthews, while Lydia Languish resembles Elizabeth Ann Linley only in her exceptional charms. The play, nevertheless, has captured the distinctive Bath atmosphere: its gallantry, its intrigue, and its gay animation. This is shown in a hundred deft touches. Rivals confront each other on the North and South Parades. "In the morning", declares Fag, the personal servant of the gallant hero Captain Absolute, "we go to the Pump Room (though neither my master nor I drink the waters); after breakfast we saunter on the Parades or play a game of billiards; at night we dance; but d——n the place, I'm tired of it; their regular hours stupefy me—not a fiddle nor a card after eleven!" The great reform of Beau Nash is recalled when Captain Absolute observes that "A sword seen in the streets of Bath would raise as great an alarm as a mad dog." The fair Lydia's maid visits a circulating library in Bath and triumphantly announces to her mistress "This is *The Gordian Knot*— and this *Peregrine Pickle*. Here are *The Tears of Sensibility*, and *Humphrey Clinker*. This is *The Memoirs of a Lady of Quality, written by herself*, and here the second volume of *The Sentimental Journey*". What more could a love-sick maiden be reasonably expected to read?

There are references to the Bath coffee-houses, and, when Captain Absolute wishes to deceive his father as to his true motives for visiting the city, he claims that he has come to recruit disbanded chairmen, minority waiters, and billiard-markers, for the army. Before the contemplated duel between Sir Lucius O'Trigger and Bob Acres, Sir Lucius cowers his opponent by asking, "Would you choose to be pickled and sent home? Or would it be the same to you to lie here in the Abbey? I'm told there is very snug lying in the Abbey." Mr. Desmond Mac-Carthy, commenting on this remark, says that "From that moment—from *The Rivals* to *John Bull's Other Island*—the Irishman who can't see a joke after he has made it has amused the English." When the *dénouement* is complete in the last act, Bob Acres cheerfully cries: "I'll order the fiddles in half an hour, to the New Rooms—and I insist on your all meeting me there." All the way through, Bath society forms the background of *The Rivals*. And its foibles and follies are accurately reflected in the characters of the play. This is also true to a large extent of Sheridan's other great comedy of manners, *The School for Scandal*, but without the same wealth of local colour. He who wishes to capture the nuances of Bath society in the later eighteenth century cannot do better than read and re-read these two plays. In that indefinable quality called "atmosphere" they are matched only by the novels of Jane Austen in the vast literature that Bath has inspired throughout the centuries.

We have seen in the previous chapter how, in the reign of Beau Nash, the most eminent literary men in the kingdom gathered under the hospitable roof of Ralph Allen at Prior Park. Unhappily this second Mæcenas had no true successor, but many would-be imitators. Chief among these was the egregious Lady Miller, wife of an Irish baronet, who lived in a villa at Batheaston some two miles from Bath. Madame D'Arblay describes her as "a round, plump, coarse-looking dame of about forty, and while all her aim is to appear an elegant woman of fashion, all her success is to seem an ordinary woman in very common life, with fine clothes on. Her movements are bustling, her air is mock-important, and her manners inelegant." In 1769 Lady Miller conceived the idea of holding weekly poetical contests at her villa. She was inspired to this end, so it appears, by discovering an antique vase at Frascati during her travels in Italy. Would not this vase be a perfect receptacle for elegant bouts-rimés? Let Horace Walpole describe the orgies that followed this discovery:

"They hold a Parnassus fair every Thursday, give out rhymes and themes, and all the flux of quality at Bath contend for the prizes. A Roman vase, dressed with pink ribands and myrtles, receives the poetry, which is drawn out every festival; six judges of these Olympic games retire and select the brightest compositions, which the respective successful acknowledge, kneel to Mrs. Calliope, kiss her fair hand, and are crowned by it with myrtle—with I don't know what. You may think this a fiction, or exaggeration. Be dumb, unbelievers! The collection is printed, published—yes, on my faith! there are bouts-rimés on a buttered muffin by Her Grace the Duchess of Northumberland, recipes to make them by Corydon the venerable, alias (George Pitt); others very pretty by Lord P(almerston), some by Lord C(armarthen), many by Mrs. M(iller) herself, that have no fault but wanting metre; and immortality promised to her without end or measure. In short, since folly, which never ripens to madness but in this climate, ran distracted, there never was anything so entertaining, or so dull—for you cannot read so long as I have been telling."

Dr. Johnson was equally emphatic in his views on Lady Miller. When Boswell named a person of his acquaintance who had written for the Vase, Johnson remarked "He was a blockhead for his pains." "The Duchess of Northumberland wrote", protested Boswell. "Sir", said Dr. Johnson, "the Duchess of Northumberland may do as she pleases: nobody will say anything to a lady of her high rank. But I should be apt to throw ——'s verses in his face." These poetical evenings went on for about twelve years and issued in the production of three volumes entitled *Poetical Amusements at a Villa near Bath*, one of the greatest monuments of literary folly in the English language. Then a curate, no longer able to endure these proceedings, sullied the purity of the sacred Vase by composing a licentious bout-rimé which threw Parnassus into confusion. Shortly afterwards Lady Miller expired at Bristol Hot Wells.

It remains to say something of the architecture of Bath in the age of Smollett and Sheridan. The most spectacular achievement of all, the Royal Crescent, dates from this period, for it was not finished until 1775. Yet spiritually and æsthetically it is unquestionably a product of the age of Beau Nash, the last and most mature achievement of that golden era. The period that we are now considering is chiefly remarkable for the building of Camden Crescent, Lansdown Crescent, the Assembly Rooms, Milsom Street, the rebuilding of the Pump Room, and the laying-out of the suburb of Bathwick. As in the former age, an uncompromising classicism is the dominant style. The ancient world still exercised an almost total sway over the minds of men.

Camden Crescent may well vie with the Royal Crescent and Prior Park for its magnificent view of the city of Bath. It was built by John Jelly and named after Lord Camden, who was a member of parliament for Bath. His coat-of-arms appears in the pediment in the centre of the crescent. An abundance of classical ornament is the prevailing feature of this group of distinguished houses.

Lansdown Crescent, the loftiest situation in Bath, bears a certain resemblance to Camden Crescent. It is a creditable piece of work, though it entirely lacks the inspiration of the Royal Crescent. The architect was John Palmer, who also built the

54   The Ionic Colonnade of the Royal Crescent,
      built by John Wood the Younger

55   The Royal Crescent, built by John Wood the Younger

quiet and dignified St. James's Square and finished the present
Pump Room.

I cannot bring myself to write about the Assembly Rooms,
those "Upper Rooms" on which the younger Wood began work
in 1771. They were almost totally destroyed in the devastating
air-raid of 1942. They were a truly wonderful set of rooms,
characterized by a severe classic dignity; the scene of many a
famous episode in real life as in literature. I pass on hastily to
Milsom Street which was built in 1762, the year after Beau
Nash's death, and rapidly became the social centre of the new
dispensation. "Milsom Street", wrote Egan during the Regency
period, "affords a most pleasant and lively residence; and
whether in or out of the Season it is highly attractive. In short,
it is the very magnet of Bath, and if there is any company
or movement in the city, Milsom Street is the pulse of it."
Architecturally, there are few lovelier sites in Bath. The gradual
declivity on which the street is built and the broadness of the
thoroughfare give it a natural dignity which is greatly enhanced by the noble appearance of the house-fronts, with their
regular classical features embellished in more than one place by
a Corinthian order of two stories. Milsom Street is the very
heart of Bath, a happy hunting-ground for social lions and
classical antiquarians.

The Pump Room, the scene of the fashionable morning
gatherings, has a somewhat complicated architectural history.
The first Pump Room, as we have seen, was erected by Beau
Nash in 1706 as part of his great "drive" to make Bath the
Mecca of Polite Society. This was greatly enlarged during the
middle years of the century. Even the enlarged building,
however, was found too small to accommodate the vast crowds
that flocked to Bath during the age of Smollett and Sheridan.
So in 1788 the architect Baldwin submitted to the City Corporation a comprehensive plan for a complete rebuilding of the
whole Pump Room area. The impressive exterior of the Pump
Room with its Ionic colonnade is almost certainly the work of
Baldwin, who afterwards had a terrific row with the Corporation
on details of design and left the project in a huff. So the completion of the interior of the Pump Room was left to John
Palmer, who finished the work in 1799. The ensemble is obviously

designed to impress the visitor. The three-quarter columns of
the Corinthian order, with richly foliated and gilded capitals,
crowned with an entablature, give the large room its essential
setting. I feel that the imitation of the ancient world has here
gone too far and over-reached itself. There is something heavy
and oppressive about the Pump Room. One is left with a
longing for the austerity of Queen Square and the spacious
simplicity of the Royal Crescent.

About the year 1770, when the popularity of Bath was so
manifestly on the increase and an unprecedented number of
people was beginning to infest the city, it was decided to build a
fashionable residential suburb in Bathwick across the Avon to
the east of the city. The first need, of course, was to bridge the
river. So certain local architects built the beautiful Pulteney
Bridge, which was named after the aristocratic landowner of
this part of the city. The architectural features of this bridge,
on which houses are built in the manner of Old London Bridge,
so that it is impossible to tell precisely when one is crossing the
river, are highly interesting. "Three high segmental arches of
equal span cross the river, the abutment at either bank standing
forward into the water. The arches are turned in single rings of
stone with a moulding worked on the face. Above this is a
plinth, upon the upper moulding of which stand the columns
and pilasters; the moulding also serves as the sill of the windows
throughout. The main cornice runs from end to end, broken only
at the central window." The houses and streets that now came
into being on the Bathwick estate of the Pulteneys were mainly
the work of Thomas Baldwin, the city architect, who was
responsible for the external features of the Pump Room. Argyle
Street, which is relatively plain and unpretentious, leads into an
irregular octagon of houses called Laura Place, which was begun
in 1788 and offers a splendid example of the best domestic
architecture of the end of the century. Ornament has here
been kept well in control. The same is true of the long and broad
Great Pulteney Street, which was built at about the same time
as Laura Place. In spite of its great length and regular features,
there is an absence of monotonous uniformity about Great
Pulteney Street. The houses are relieved by fluted pilasters and
pediments mark the limits of each well-defined group. The

56   The Royal and Lansdown Crescents in 1819:   from a plate by W. Watts

57   Pulteney Bridge and the River Avon

Adam influence is here very evident. The Holburne or Menstrie Museum (once the Sydney Hotel) stands at the end of Great Pulteney Street with its imposing façade of Corinthian columns and general appearance of well-bred elegance. The rest of Bathwick is in the same tradition: noble, refined, aristocratic, fully consonant to a city which deemed exclusiveness as the highest virtue at the very time when it was being invaded by the mob.

On the general features of eighteenth-century architecture in Bath we may turn to the considered judgment of Mowbray Green:

"Speaking generally, the style of the 18th century may be divided into three groups—that of the first 25 years, when the houses had gabled roofs and façades with large sash windows surrounded by bolection mouldings, and when the interiors were panelled, and the rooms small and comfortable; the next 50 years, when the work was modelled on the classic Palladian manner with a rusticated basement, a two-storeyed order, a crowning cornice and parapet, with a Mansard or curb roof over, while the interior became spacious and dignified, and plaster work was brought into general use; and the last 25 years, when the free manner of Robert Adam came into vogue, and the strong methods of the earlier times gave way to detailed and abundant decoration." So at Bath we have epitomized, as it were in microcosm, the whole of the architectural history of England in the eighteenth century. Such dignity, such charm, such grandeur and magnificence as Bath possessed, richly qualified the city of Beau Nash for the honorary title of Queen of the West.

6

The Bath of Jane Austen

THE TRANSFORMATION OF BATH, THE MECCA OF GAY BIRDS of passage, into the last refuge for half-pay officers and retired civil servants was a long and gradual process. There are three logical stages in this process, none of which can be fitted into an exact time-sequence. First of all, as we have seen, Bath became the metropolis of the world of fashion under Beau Nash. Then the middle classes and the multitude pursued the fashionable and the exclusive to Bath and delighted in apeing their manners. This was going on during all that period which we have called the age of Smollett and Sheridan. Finally, at the end of the eighteenth century and the beginning of the following century, disintegrating elements destroyed the society of Bath from within. The Pump Room and the Assembly Rooms, which were besieged by Tom, Dick, and Harry, ceased to be the centres of Polite Society. Private and exclusive parties took their place. This spelt the end. When Jane Austen wrote in *Persuasion* (1816) that "The theatre or the rooms . . . were not fashionable enough for the Elliots, whose evening amusements were solely in the elegant stupidity of private parties", she was pronouncing the death-knell of Bath society and of everything for which Beau Nash had lived and worked. Within twenty years of her writing Bath had become a place of permanent residence and retirement for admirals, generals, civil servants, and clergymen of all denominations. The glories of the reign of the Beau were but a distant memory.

The company at Bath in the last decades of the eighteenth century, as portrayed by Smollett and caricatured by Anstey, had lost any pretence of exclusiveness. "Here we have Ministers of State, judges, generals, bishops, projectors, philosophers, wits, poets, players, chemists, fiddlers, and buffoons", wrote Jerry Melford to his friend the Oxford don in *Humphry Clinker*. The Pump Room must have resembled a cattle-market and the Assembly Rooms appeared more like a circus than the rendez-

vous of the *élite*. When the season ended Jerry Melford noticed
that "all our gay birds of passage have taken their flight to
Bristol Well, Tunbridge, Brighthelmstone, Scarborough, Harrow-
gate, etc. Not a soul is seen in this place, but a few broken-
winded parsons, waddling about like so many crows along the
North Parade. There is always a great show of the clergy at
Bath; none of your thin, puny, yellow, hectic figures, exhausted
with abstinence and hard study, labouring under the *morbi
eruditorum*; but great overgrown dignitaries and rectors, with
rubicund noses and gouty ancles, or broad bloated faces, drag-
ging along great swag bellies; the emblems of sloth and in-
digestion." Shades of Beau Nash!

If the Bath of the last quarter of the eighteenth century
is mirrored to perfection in *The Rivals* of Sheridan, the *fin de
siècle* and the years after Waterloo are portrayed with exquisite
artistry and subtle irony by Jane Austen in *Northanger Abbey*
and *Persuasion*. "The visits of Jane Austen to Bath", Miss
Austen-Leigh tells us, "probably began at an early age when
she would have stayed with her Leigh Perrot or Cooper relations."
Mr. Leigh Perrot was a brother of Mrs. Austen and the victim of
acute attacks of gout which occasioned frequent visits to Bath.
His family circle foregathered at No. 1, Paragon. Mrs. Cooper
was a sister of Mrs. Austen and settled at Bath when her husband
gave up his rectory. The first recorded visit of Jane Austen to
Bath was in 1797 when she probably stayed at Paragon. We
know that she arrived in Bath on a gloomy day, which she may
well have had in mind when recording the arrival of Lady
Russell and Anne Elliot at Bath in *Persuasion* some twenty
years later:

"When Lady Russell, not long afterwards, was entering Bath
on a wet afternoon, and driving through the long courses of
streets from the Old Bridge to Camden Place (i.e. the Camden
Crescent of to-day), amidst the dash of other carriages, the
heavy rumble of carts and drays, the bawling of newsmen,
muffin-men and milk-men, and the ceaseless clink of pattens,
she made no complaint. No, these were noises which belonged
to the winter pleasures; her spirits rose under their influence.
. . . Anne did not share these feelings. She persisted in a very
determined, though very silent, disinclination for Bath; caught

the first dim view of the extensive buildings, smoking in rain, without any wish of seeing them better; felt their progress through the streets to be, however disagreeable, yet too rapid; for who would be glad to see her when she arrived? And looked back, with fond regret, to the bustles of Uppercross and the seclusion of Kellynch."

Jane Austen was at Bath again in 1799, when she spent several weeks in Queen Square. This situation greatly pleased her, as it would any person of cultivated taste. She told her sister Cassandra that "it is far more cheerful than Paragon, and the prospect from the drawing-room window, at which I now write, is rather picturesque, as it commands a prospective view of the left side of Brock Street, broken by three Lombardy poplars in the garden of the last house in Queen Square."

She attended the festivities in Sydney Gardens (the Bath equivalent of Vauxhall Gardens) and thoroughly enjoyed the gaiety and bustle of the city after her quiet life in the rectory at Steventon.

In the year 1800 Jane's father, the Rev. George Austen, gave up his living in Hampshire and retired with his family to Bath. At first Jane did not welcome the change, and "for a time (says Miss Austen Leigh) she was very unhappy. She loved Steventon and all that it meant to her. The Rectory had been her home for twenty-five years. Here she had shared a happy family life with brothers now out in the world, and had enjoyed years of pleasant intercourse with neighbours and friends, rich and poor. Here too she had discovered her gift for writing." Gradually, however, Jane learnt to adjust herself to the new way of life. At first she and her mother stayed with the Leigh Perrots and then in June 1801 the whole family settled at No. 4, Sydney Place, a quiet secluded house near the far end of Great Pulteney Street on the Bathwick estate. Early in 1805 the family was tragically bereaved by the death of the father and in the following year Jane and her mother and sisters left Bath never to return. Jane was never really fond of the city. In July 1808 she wrote to her sister, "It will be two years to-morrow since we left Bath for Clifton, with what happy feelings of escape!" Yet in these five years' residence at Bath Jane learnt much in her own demure unobtrusive manner about human behaviour that

58   The Slopes leading to Lansdown Crescent

59   Camden Crescent, built by John Jelly

60   Lansdown Crescent, built by John Palmer: from a plate by A. Woodroffe (*ca.* 1820)

served her in very good stead when writing those novels which will ever rank among the great imperishable literature of this country. She by no means shrank from those social pleasures which Bath still offered to all who were prepared to forget their dignity and position and to enjoy the society of their fellow human beings. Shortly after she had arrived in Bath we find Jane writing to Cassandra:

"In the evening I hope you honoured my Toilette and Ball with a thought; I dressed myself as well as I could, and had all my finery much admired at home. By nine o'clock my Uncle, Aunt and I entered the Rooms and linked Miss Winstone on to us. Before tea it was rather a dull affair; but then the 'before tea' did not last long, for there was only one dance, danced by four couple. Think of four couple, surrounded by about an hundred people, dancing in the Upper Rooms at Bath! After tea, we *cheered* up; the breaking up of private parties sent some scores more to the Ball, and tho' it was shockingly and inhumanly thin for this place, there were people enough, I suppose, to have made five or six very pretty Basingstoke assemblies." The reference in this letter to private parties is very interesting; it shows that Society at Bath was still in a transition period, attempting to make the best of both the world of private and exclusive intercourse and the world of official and public assemblies.

The best proof that Jane Austen was not unmoved by the Bath scene, from which she manifestly derived a great deal of shy and quite unmalicious amusement, is to be found in the two great novels which portray this society with such minute fidelity. *Northanger Abbey* and *Persuasion* contain no "set-pieces" of descriptive imagination, no grand attempt to view the city as a whole in a single panorama. It is in their incidental allusions to Bath topography, in their exact delineation of the common events of daily life, that these novels achieve their astonishing actuality.

Northanger Abbey comes first. It was written during the year 1798, though not published until twenty years later. That one truly innocent girl of English fiction, Catherine Morland, who "had reached the age of seventeen without having seen one amiable youth who could call forth her sensibility" is launched into "all the difficulties and dangers of a six weeks' residence in Bath". She went in the company of Mr. Allen, a sensible intelligent man, and Mrs. Allen, an empty, vain, and garrulous woman, who displayed far more interest in her dress and coiffure than the pleasures of her youthful guest. They found comfortable lodgings in Great Pulteney Street (which had only just been built) and sought the first convenient opportunity of visiting the Upper Rooms. The visit, however, was a failure, for they knew no one in Bath and were ignored by the gay throng. The mornings offered no more consolation in the way of company. "Every morning now brought its regular duties—shops were to be visited; some new part of the town to be looked at; and the Pump Room to be attended, where they paraded up and down for an hour, looking at every body and speaking to no one." The spell was broken at last when they visited the Lower Rooms. The Master of the Ceremonies introduced Catherine to "a very gentlemanlike young man as a partner;—his name was Tilney. He seemed to be about four or five and twenty, was rather tall, had a pleasing countenance, a very intelligent and lively eye, and, if not quite handsome, was very near to it. His address was good, and Catherine felt herself in high luck." He was, in fact, a country clergyman in Gloucestershire, the younger son of General Tilney of Northanger Abbey. In jest he proceeded to ply Catherine with the usual questions.

"After chatting some time on such matters as naturally arose from the objects around them, he suddenly addressed her with—'I have hitherto been very remiss, madam, in the proper attentions of a partner here; I have not yet asked you how long you have been in Bath; whether you were ever here before; whether you have been at the Upper Rooms, the theatre, and the concert; and how you like the place altogether. I have been very negligent—but are you now at leisure to satisfy me in these particulars. If you are I will begin directly.'

" 'You need not give yourself that trouble, sir.'

" 'No trouble, I assure you, madam.' Then forming his features into a set smile, and affectedly softening his voice, he added, with a simpering air, 'Have you been long in Bath, madam?'

" 'About a week, sir,' replied Catherine, trying not to laugh.

" 'Really!' with affected astonishment.

A PEEP into the PUMP ROOM or the Somersetshire folk in a Maze.

61   Pump Room Characters of 1818

62, 63, 64 Bath Windows and Balconies

" 'Why should you be surprised, sir?'

" 'Why, indeed?' said he, in his natural tone—'but some emotion must appear to be raised by your reply, and surprise is more easily assumed, and not less reasonable, than any other. —Now let us go on. Were you never here before, madam?'

" ' Never, sir.'

" 'Indeed! Have you yet honoured the Upper Rooms?'

" 'Yes, sir, I was there last Monday.'

" 'Have you been to the theatre?'

" 'Yes, sir, I was at the play on Tuesday.'

" 'To the concert?'

" 'Yes, sir, on Wednesday.'

" 'And are you altogether pleased with Bath?'

" 'Yes—I like it very well.'

" 'Now I must give one smirk, and then we may be rational again.' "

The greater part of the story deals with the slowly maturing love of Catherine and Henry. The scene of this romance is laid first at Bath, then at Northanger Abbey, while the final *dénouement* and declarations of eternal fidelity take place at Catherine's home in Wiltshire. Variety is lent to the Bath picture by the appearance of an old friend of Mrs. Allen, a certain Mrs. Thorpe, with her son John, her daughter Isabella, and two younger daughters. Isabella Thorpe is a vain coquette who uses the friendship of Catherine for her own ends. The relations of this pair lead to many scenes described with that quiet irony of which Jane Austen was such a consummate master. One morning when they were in the Pump Room together, Isabella hastily exclaimed, " 'For Heaven's sake! let us move away from this end of the room. Do you know, there are two odious young men who have been staring at me this half hour. They really put me quite out of countenance. Let us go and look at the arrivals. They will hardly follow us there.'

"Away they walked to the book; and while Isabella examined the names, it was Catherine's employment to watch the proceedings of these alarming young men.

" 'They are not coming this way, are they? I hope they are not so impertinent as to follow us. Pray let me know if they are coming. I am determined I will not look up.'

"In a few moments Catherine, with unaffected pleasure, assured her that she need no longer be uneasy, as the gentlemen had just left the Pump Room.

" 'And which way are they gone?' said Isabella, turning hastily round. 'One was a very good-looking young man.'

" 'They went towards the churchyard.'

" 'Well, I am amazingly glad I have got rid of them! And now, what say you to going to Edgar's Buildings with me, and looking at my new hat? You said you should like to see it.'

"Catherine readily agreed. 'Only,' she added, 'perhaps we may overtake the two young men.'

" 'Oh, never mind that. If we make haste, we shall pass by them presently, and I am dying to shew you my hat.'

" 'But if we only wait a few minutes, there will be no danger of our seeing them at all.'

" 'I shall not pay them any such compliment, I assure you. I have no notion of treating men with such respect. *That* is the way to spoil them.'

"Catherine had nothing to oppose against such reasoning; and therefore, to show the independence of Miss Thorpe, and her resolution of humbling the sex, they set off immediately as fast as they could walk, in pursuit of the two young men."

In spite of being detained on the way, Isabella Thorpe had her hope fulfilled and "so pure and uncoquettish were her feelings, that, though they overtook and passed the two offending young men in Milsom Street, she was so far from seeking to attract their notice, that she looked back at them only three times."

The Pump Room and its animated company appear constantly in the pages of *Northanger Abbey*. One Sunday the Thorpes and the Allens joined the throng there after church, but only "to discover that the crowd was insupportable, and that there was not a genteel face to be seen, which everybody discovers every Sunday throughout the season". Isabella Thorpe had her favourite seat in the Pump Room. " 'This is my favourite place,' said she, as they sat down on a bench between the doors, which commanded a tolerable view of everybody entering at either, 'it is so out of the way'." The chosen resort of the *élite* was now the Royal Crescent, whither the Allens and Thorpes

65   The Milsom Street of Jane Austen : from a plate by A. Woodroffe (*ca.* 1820)

hastily repaired "to breathe the fresh air of better company" when the Pump Room revealed not a genteel face. Reference is made to "the afternoon's Crescent" as a regular item in the social routine of the period. On one celebrated occasion Henry Tilney and his sister Eleanor took Catherine for a walk round Beechen Cliff "that noble hill, whose beautiful verdure and hanging coppice render it so striking an object from almost every opening in Bath". They discussed the merits of Mrs. Radcliffe's tale of horror, *The Mysteries of Udolpho,* to which Catherine was passionately addicted, and went on to debate how "real solemn history" was written. Then Henry, who was in a very lively mood, gave Catherine a lecture on drawing and perspective. "He talked of fore-grounds, distances, and second distances—side-screens and perspectives—lights and shades;—and Catherine was so hopeful a scholar, that when they gained the top of Beechen Cliff, she voluntarily rejected the whole city of Bath as unworthy to make part of a landscape". Not long after this walk the Tilneys and Catherine left Bath for Northanger Abbey and the romance proceeds to its inevitable conclusion.

In *Persuasion,* which was finished in 1816, some twenty years later than *Northanger Abbey,* we find ourselves once more in Bath, "but (as Miss Austen-Leigh so truly observes), it is Bath with a difference . . . the spirit of Bath seems to have changed. Its attraction as a centre of fashion has begun to wane. The star of Brighton has arisen, thanks to the favour of the Regent, and a new centre been created for the idle, the rich, and the fashionable. Many of them still visit Bath, but they are apt to shun the public balls and assemblies and to despise the mixed crowds that now throng them. The old days of the dictatorial Masters of the Ceremonies are gone and the fashion of private parties among the more select of the visitors has spread." The novel, which in my judgment is the most mature and masterly of Jane Austen's works, gives a delightful picture of Bath society in the year after the Napoleonic Wars when many senior officers, suddenly driven ashore by the conclusion of peace, determined to make it their place of permanent residence. Bath also became the place of permanent residence for such as Sir Walter Elliot, an impoverished Somerset landowner, who found that, as compared with London (the only possible alternative for a person of his standing), "it was a much safer place for a gentleman in his predicament:—he might there be important at comparatively little expense." So Sir Walter Elliot and his insufferable daughter Elizabeth took up residence at "a very good house in Camden Place (*i.e.*, Camden Crescent), a lofty, dignified situation, such as becomes a man of consequence", where they were later joined by the younger daughter Anne, the heroine of the story.

The characters move in a graceful tranquil way among the streets, squares, and crescents of Bath. Lady Russell, whose great respect for rank and consequence could not entirely conceal a warm and generous heart, had her lodgings in Rivers Street at a short distance from the Elliots. Lady Dalrymple and her daughter, the relations of whom Sir Walter made so much, "had taken a house, for three months, in Laura Place, and would be living in style"—further evidence of the exclusive character of the new Bathwick estate. Mrs. Smith, an old school-friend of Anne Elliot, who had suffered much from the slings and arrows of outrageous fortune, lived in the unfashionable Westgate Buildings. There she was visited by Anne, much to the chagrin of Sir Walter. " 'Westgate Buildings!' said he, 'and who is Miss Anne Elliot to be visiting in Westgate Buildings?' " Sir Walter, quite apart from his absurd class consciousness, had a poor view of the women of Bath.

"The worst of Bath was the number of its plain women. He did not mean to say that there were no pretty women, but the number of the plain was out of all proportion. He had frequently observed, as he walked, that one handsome face would be followed by thirty, or five and thirty frights; and once, as he had stood in a shop in Bond Street, he had counted eighty-seven women go by, one after another, without there being a tolerable face among them."

Would Sir Walter Elliot fare better to-day if he returned to his vantage-point in Bath?

Admiral Croft, the tenant of Kellynch Hall, Sir Walter's residence in Somerset, came with his wife to Bath to take the waters and lodged in Gay Street. " 'I suspect,' said Sir Walter coolly, 'that Admiral Croft will be best known in Bath as the renter of Kellynch Hall. Elizabeth, may we venture to present him and his wife in Laura Place?' 'Oh no, I think not. Situated as we are with Lady Dalrymple, cousins, we ought to be very careful not to embarrass her with acquaintance she might not approve. If we were not related it would not signify; but as cousins, she would feel scrupulous as to any proposal of ours. We had better leave the Crofts to find their own level. There are several odd-looking men walking about here, who, I am told, are sailors. The Crofts will associate with them.'" The Crofts, it is to be feared, had little reverence for Sir Walter or even interest in the acquaintance. They "considered their intercourse with the Elliots as a mere matter of form, and not in the least likely to afford them any pleasure." We are given a most vivid picture of disbanded naval officers settling in Bath after the Napoleonic Wars. Anne Elliot always watched the Crofts as long as she could, "delighted to fancy she understood what they might be talking of, as they walked along in happy independence, or equally delighted to see the Admiral's hearty shake of the hand when he encountered an old friend, and observe their eagerness of conversation when occasionally forming into a little knot of the navy, Mrs. Croft looking as intelligent and keen as any of the officers around her."

Then there is the delightful incident of Anne's meeting with Admiral Croft in Milsom Street:

"Anne was too much engaged with Lady Russell to be often walking herself, but it so happened one morning, about a week or ten days after the Crofts' arrival, it suited her best to leave her friend, or her friend's carriage, in the lower part of the town, and return alone to Camden Place; and in walking up Milsom Street, she had the good fortune to meet with the Admiral. He was standing by himself, at a printshop window, with his hands behind him, in earnest contemplation of some print, and she not only might have passed him unseen, but was obliged to touch as well as address him before she could catch his notice. When he did perceive and acknowledge her, however, it was done with all his usual frankness and good humour. 'Ha! is it you? Thank you, thank you. This is treating me like a friend. Here I am, you see, staring at a picture. I can never get by this shop without stopping. But what a thing here is, by way of a boat! Do look at it. Did you ever see the like? What queer fellows your fine painters must be, to think that any body would

venture their lives in such a shapeless old cockle-shell as that?
And yet here are two gentlemen stuck up in it mightily at their
ease, and looking about them at the rocks and mountains, as if
they were not to be upset the next moment, which they certainly
must be. I wonder where that boat was built!' (laughing
heartily). 'I would not venture over a horsepond in it. Well,'
(turning away), 'now, where are you bound? Can I go any
where for you, or with you? Can I be of any use?'

"'None, I thank you, unless you will give me the pleasure of
your company the little way our road lies together. I am going
home.' 'That I will, with all my heart, and farther too. Yes, yes,
we will have a snug walk together. . . . There, take my arm;
that's right; I do not feel comfortable if I have not a woman
there. Lord! what a boat it is!' taking a last look at the picture,
as they began to be in motion.''

A still more celebrated occasion is the meeting in Milsom Street
of the heroine Anne Elliot with the hero, Captain Frederick
Wentworth, who all unknown to her had come to Bath to solicit
her hand. It had just begun to rain and Anne Elliot, who was in
Milsom Street with her sister and cousin and Mrs. Clay, had
taken refuge in a shop called Molland's. "Anne, as she sat near
the window, descried most decidedly and distinctly, Captain
Wentworth, walking down the street. Her start was perceptible
only to herself; but she instantly felt that she was the greatest
simpleton in the world, the most unaccountable and absurd!
For a few minutes she saw nothing before her. It was all confusion. She was lost; and when she had scolded back her senses,
she found the others still waiting for the carriage, and Mr. Elliot
(always obliging), just setting off for Union Street on a commission of Mrs. Clay's.''

"She now felt a great inclination to go to the outer door; she
wanted to see if it rained. Why was she to suspect herself of
another motive? Captain Wentworth must be out of sight.
She left her seat, she would go, one half of her should not be
always so much wiser than the other half, or always suspecting
the other of being worse than it was. She would see if it rained.
She was sent back, however, in a moment by the entrance of
Captain Wentworth himself, among a party of gentlemen and
ladies, evidently his acquaintance, and whom he must have

66   Lansdown Tower, Beckford's last Folly, overlooking Bath, built in
1822: from a lithograph by Willes Maddox (1844)

joined a little below Milsom Street. He was more obviously struck and confused by the sight of her, than he had ever observed before; he looked quite red. For the first time, since their renewed acquaintance, she felt that she was betraying the least sensibility of the two. She had the advantage of him, in the preparation of the last few moments. All the overpowering, blinding, bewildering, first effects of strong surprise were over with her. Still, however, she had enough to feel! It was agitation, pain, pleasure, a something between delight and misery."

From this moment the story concerns itself almost solely with the love of Anne for Captain Wentworth and of Captain Wentworth for Anne, until at last he declares that love in a letter written in extreme agitation in the White Hart Hotel (which occupied the site of the grandiose structure which goes to-day by the name of the Grand Pump Room Hotel). The final scene is laid in Union Street just below Milsom Street. Captain Wentworth was at last alone with Anne, free from all unwelcome company and well-meaning escorts.

"Soon words enough had passed between them to decide their direction towards the comparatively quiet and retired gravel walk, where the power of conversation would make the present hour a blessing indeed, and prepare it for all the immortality which the happiest recollections of their own future lives could bestow. There they exchanged again those feelings and those promises which had once before seemed to secure everything, but which had been followed by so many, many years of division and estrangement. There they returned again into the past, more exquisitely happy, perhaps, in their reunion, than when it had first been projected; more tender, more tried, more fixed in a knowledge of each other's character, truth, and attachment; more equal to act, more justified in acting. And there, as they slowly paced the gradual ascent, heedless of every group around them, seeing neither sauntering politicians, bustling house-keepers, flirting girls, nor nursery-maids and children, they could indulge in those retrospections and acknowledgements, and especially in those explanations of what had directly preceded the present moment, which were so poignant and so ceaseless in interest. All the little variations of the last week were gone through; and of yesterday and to-day there could scarcely be an end."

Jane Austen's Bath, then, is a city in a state of transition from a resort of fashion and pleasure into a place of permanent residence for gentlemen like Sir Walter Elliot, (who could not afford the much greater expenditure that society in London demanded), for half-pay officers, and for retired clergymen. We feel, at times, in reading Jane Austen, that we are on the threshold of the long sober Victorian era. Elegance is beginning to give way to respectability. If, however, we turn to a work that is strictly contemporary with *Persuasion*, namely, *Egan's Walks Through Bath* (1819), we can see that Bath society still had its charms and allurements. Listen to his description of Milsom Street:

"All is bustle and gaiety: numerous dashing equipages passing and repassing, others gracing the doors of the tradesmen; sprinkled here and there with the invalids in the comfortable sedans and easy two-wheeled carriages, all anxious to participate in this active part of Bath, giving a sort of finish to the scene."

Then go to the Royal Crescent:

"At all times it is an attractive promenade for the visitors of Bath ; but in the season, of a Sunday, it is also crowded with fashionables of every rank; and with the addition of the splendid barouche, dashing curricle, elegant tandem, gentlemen on horseback, etc., the Royal Crescent strongly reminds the spectator of Hyde Park, Rotten Row, and Kensington Gardens, when adorned with all their brilliancy of company."

It is true that when Egan entered the Abbey, he found that "a pleasing melancholy pervades the frame" (a very eighteenth-century sentiment, not at all characteristic of the Regency!) but when he arrived in his "Aquatic Stroll"—as he pompously terms it—at Avon Street he was more in his element.

"Avon Street, the receptacle for unfortunate women, calls forth very different sensations: and although it may be termed the *Wapping* of Bath, it is but common justice to observe that it is far removed from the disgusting scenes which are so publicly witnessed at this memorable place at the east end of the metropolis. With all the vigilance of the police of this elegant City and its active Corporation towards removing public nuisances, Bath, in

67   The Circulating Library in Milsom Street: from a print of 1829

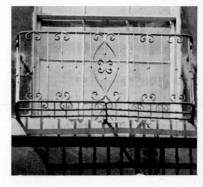

68-73   Regency Balconies in Bath

the height of its season, has its share of the *frail sisterhood*; but their language, manners, and demeanour, are not of that very obtrusive nature which characterize these unhappy females in London, Liverpool, and Dublin. Houses of *ill-fame* (or if a more genteel phrase is acceptable, in the term BAGNIOS, for such houses) are to be discovered in Bath. Upon the *search-nights*, which generally commence with much activity upon the accession of a new Mayor into office, some females of rather a higher caste, with their amorous gallants, have been obliged to acknowledge or show a sort of passport, to account for their *awkward* situations, before they could obtain a *discharge* the next morning." I need hardly say that none of Jane Austen's characters ever ventured in the neighbourhood of Avon Street!

While Bath offered every variety of pleasure to the rich, Holloway, just over the Old Bath Bridge, was frequented by beggars and outcasts. Professor Earle writes:

"In proportion as the Squares and Crescents filled with the affluent, the dens of Holloway filled with beggars. This was their camp, from whence they watched the visitors who were their prey, and eluded the Corporation who were their natural enemies. Holloway was outside the jurisdiction of the borough and beyond the control of the bye-laws. So there they had their nocturnal entertainment, and by day they distributed themselves through the streets of Bath. Mendicants were at this time exceedingly numerous all through the country, and they were much complained of, but Bath, which enjoyed a pre-eminence in other things, was equally distinguished for its colony of beggars.

"Holloway was a parody of Bath. As the fine shops of Bath got in their new and fashionable goods at the approach of the Season, so the petty chandlers of Holloway who traded with the Bath shopkeepers were constantly found to double their orders at the same epoch. As the price of lodgings varied in Bath according to an understood attraction, so in Holloway was there a like variety offered to the selection of the professional beggar."

In forming a balanced picture of Bath in its heyday and decline, we must always remember Avon Street and Holloway. They are eloquent of much in the history of Bath that is best unrecorded.

14

BATH

A symbol of the change in Bath society from the ultra-fashionable to the ultra-respectable is the substitution of the bath-chair for the sedan-chair as the mode of conveyance for invalids. This dates from the second and third decades of the nineteenth century. Here is the tariff for sedan-chairs fixed by the mayor and two justices and printed in Egan's *Walks Through Bath* (1819):

	s.	d.
For carrying one person any distance not exceeding 500 yards	0	6
Above 500, and not exceeding 1173 yards	1	0
Beyond 1173 yards, and not exceeding one mile	1	6
Beyond one measured mile, and not exceeding in the whole one mile and 586 yards	2	0
Not exceeding one mile, 1173 yards	2	6
Not exceeding two measured miles	3	0
And for every 586 yards beyond	0	6

Any person may detain the chairmen in every fare, without paying anything for it, as follows, viz:

	Minutes		*Minutes*
In a sixpenny fare	10	In a two shilling fare	25
In a twelvepenny fare	15	In a half-a-crown fare	30
In an eighteenpenny fare	20	In a three shilling fare	35

And in every other fare or quantity of ground constituting an additional fare, any farther time not exceeding in each additional sixpenny fare, as above, five minutes.

All fares to be charged double after twelve o'clock at night. And, instead of 500 yards, 300 are only a sixpenny fare on hilly or ascending ground, whether upwards or downwards; but where the fare begins on plain ground, and ends on ascent, or begins on a descent and ends on plain ground, the chairmen must carry the full space of 500 yards.

Chairmen to be paid 6d. for each extra quarter of an hour's waiting. Chairmen demanding more for their fare than they are entitled to, or refusing or declining to carry any fare when called on, or using any abusive or insulting language, shall forfeit 20s., or be suspended from using their chair for any time not exceeding forty days.

The mayor and two justices to direct the measurement of any distances in dispute, the expense of which to be paid by the chairmen, if the distance be less than they charge, and, if more, by the persons they carry.

By the accession of Queen Victoria, 1837, the sedan-chairs had all disappeared from the streets, squares, and crescents of

106

Bath. The bath-chairs, dull, monotonous, respectable, were to be seen everywhere in all their cold and drab unloveliness.

In 1823, when the Victorian age was already looming in the near future, an extraordinary figure took up his residence at Bath. William Beckford might have sprung straight from the pages of the *Arabian Nights*. His rich and luxurious oriental imagination made him an astonishing anomaly to a generation which was rapidly subordinating good taste and elegance to a formidable mass of stuffy social conventions. The author of *Vathek* and the creator of the Gothic follies of Fonthill Abbey was unlikely to be *persona grata* in the best Bath society. The man who dreamt of the Mountain of the Four Fountains, the flowery meadows of Rocnabad, and the holy besom of Mecca, was unlikely to have a very sensitive appreciation of the Railway Age and the Age of Iron and Steel.

The Abbot of Fonthill, as Beckford was commonly called, purchased two houses in Lansdown Crescent. Local gossip at once became busy. "Exotic and unholy rites, it was well known, took place nightly behind those crimson curtains, through which the streaming light cast a baleful echo on the pavement." Beckford saw fit to identify himself with Vathek, went everywhere with a misshapen dwarf by the name of Perro, and called his house Bagdad. A recent biographer has recaptured the quaint spectacle of Beckford's cavalcade. "At the head rode the steward . . . two grooms followed, armed with long whips; then, in the midst of half-a-dozen dogs, the Caliph, on his grey Arab, a thin, morose figure, survival of the eighteenth century, in his top-boots, knee-breeches, green coat, frill and white neck-cloth; while two more grooms brought up the rear." The Abbot of Fonthill soon found means of self-expression and a chance of gratifying his exotic tastes. On the crest of Lansdown Hill there was a tract of waste land. Beckford purchased this and raised Lansdown Tower, one of the curiosities of English architecture. It was some 130 feet high and crowned with a cast-iron model of the temple of Lysicrates. "High up lay a large square apartment, lighted by twelve windows and hung with scarlet curtains, whence the Bristol Channel could be scanned and the country eastwards as far as his abandoned spire (of Fonthill). Lower down, a door led to a small vaulted corridor, where stood

Rossi's St. Anthony, backed by a slab of red porphyry, and flanked by Perugino's 'Virgin' and Raphael's 'St. Catherine', whilst a rich cabinet housed the more precious of his religious manuscripts. Beyond lay another apartment, where hung Bellini's 'Doge Loredarno', some Polembergs and a Hondekoeter farmyard, facing a collection of cabinets, candlesticks, vases, cups, jewels and marbles." This luxurious folly has, by an odd metamorphosis, been recently converted into an Anglican chapel.

The Abbot of Fonthill lived at Bath until his death in 1844. He achieved what is given to so few: he became a legend in his own lifetime. The people of Bath viewed him with a mixture of fear, awe, and wonderment. This aloof mysterious figure seemed to have escaped from an age infinitely remote from their own. When men saw him in the Bath bookshops, or with his strange cavalcade of followers, they shrank back in holy fear and dread. Superb anachronism as he was, with his pale shade expired the very last flicker of the eighteenth century.

The last phase in the social history of Bath is the visit of Mr. Pickwick, who was received by Angelo Cyrus Bantam, Master of the Ceremonies. Charles Dickens does full justice to the occasion: "'Mr. Pickwick,' said Dowler, 'my friend, Angelo Cyrus Bantam, Esquire, M.C. Bantam, Mr. Pickwick. Know each other. Welcome to Ba-ath, sir. This is indeed an acquisition. Most welcome to Ba-ath, sir. It is long, very long, Mr. Pickwick, since you drank the waters. It appears an age, Mr. Pickwick. Re-markable!' Such were the expressions with which Angelo Cyrus Bantam, Esquire, M.C., took Mr. Pickwick's hand; retaining it in his meantime, and shrugging up his shoulders with a constant succession of bows, as if he really could not make up his mind to the trial of letting it go again. 'It is a very long time since I drank the waters, certainly,' replied Mr. Pickwick, 'for, to the best of my knowledge, I was never here before'." This was followed by a visit to the Assembly Rooms, where Mr. Pickwick played his celebrated game of whist. But the scene is one of vanished splendour, and an anonymous poet of this period might well lament:

"No seats for peeresses are now appointed,
But rank and title are all disjointed.
And ev'ry upstart whom Great Nash had humbled
With dukes and princes, counts and lords, is jumbled."

74   Early Victorian Bath: the Market Place and Guildhall

75, 76   St. James's Square: the old Paving and Dickens's House

77, 78   Bath Steps and Pavements

79, 80, 81   Georgian and Later Monuments in the Abbey Church

The truth is, of course, that with the greatly increased facilities for travel and the wider diffusion of wealth, Fashionable Society had migrated abroad to the foreign spas which had become international resorts. As M. Barbeau has succinctly expressed it:

"A sojourn on the banks of the Avon ceased to be the almost classic *villegiatura*, the first and almost the only one that suggested itself, the one that was naturally, almost necessarily, associated with the idea of holidays and change of air. A hundred other places, hitherto inaccessible or unknown to the crowd, competed for the various groups which the old social attraction of Bath was gradually ceasing to muster there. To say nothing of rivals that had long remained obscure, like Cheltenham, but which became suddenly popular, as more rural and less commonplace, Paris, Italy, the traditional goals of the English traveller, invited the British multitude. The new-born lovers of wild and picturesque nature turned to the Alps, sung by Byron; the mountains of Scotland, extolled by Scott; the English Lakes, immortalized by Wordsworth. The recently created vogue of seaside resorts peopled the coast, and filled Brighton and Boulogne.

"Even the first and fundamental *clientèle* of Bath, the invalids, dwindled; delicate persons found the air of Torquay or Cannes milder; the German baths offered greater comfort, prices probably lower, and above all, a more complete change of air and habits, to sufferers.

"If these German resorts, Homburg and Baden, to which we may add Spa, replaced the ancient Bath that was disappearing, in the affections of the English generally, and not only in those of the invalids, it was because in many points they reproduced it with added splendour and on a larger scale. They had the same social brilliance, enhanced indeed by the fact that their visitors were not confined to the English aristocracy, but included that of every continental country. Play was high at these places, roulette and trente-et-quarante falling in no wise short of Nash's EO and faro. Finally, and this was by no means the least of all these attractions, morals were not severe, and the libertines of both sexes did not feel themselves supervised, as in England, by a public opinion that had become rigorous, and harassed by a Press that revelled in the denunciation of scandals.

Invalids, pleasure-seekers, gamblers, adventurers, gathered there as formerly on the banks of the Avon, and led a very similar life in surroundings that were much the same."

The later nineteenth century saw a lot of ribbon development in Bath, a great deal of inferior building which still disgraces the outskirts of the city and mars its unity of style and feeling. Recently however the Bath Corporation has, in its wisdom, seen fit to decree that all building in the city shall be of Bath stone and consonant to the architectural style of the eighteenth century. So we may fondly hope that further enormities will be ruthlessly prohibited.

I like to take leave of Bath, as I picture it to-day, in the beautiful lines of Swinburne, so richly eloquent of a city truly tranquil, at peace with itself, its historic mission fulfilled:

> "Like a queen enchanted that may not laugh nor weep,
> Glad at heart and guarded from change and care like ours,
> Girt about with beauty by days and nights that creep
> Soft as breathless ripples that softly shorewards sweep,
> Lies the lovely city whose grace no grief deflowers.
> Age and grey forgetfulness, time that shifts and veers,
> Touch not thee, our fairest, whose charm no rival nears,
> Hailed as England's Florence of one whose praise gives grace,
> Landor, once thy lover, a name that love reveres:
> Dawn and noon and sunset are one before they face."

> "Dawn whereof we know not, and noon whose fruit we reap,
> Garnered up in record of years that fell like flowers,
> Sunset liker sunrise along the shining steep
> Whence thy fair face lightens, and where thy soft springs leap,
> Crown at once and gird thee with grace of guardian powers.
> Loved of men beloved of us, souls that fame inspheres,
> All thine air hath music for him who dreams and hears,
> Voices mixed of multitudes, feet of friends that pace,
> Witness why for ever, if heaven's face clouds or clears,
> Dawn and noon and sunset are one before they face."

> "Peace has here found harbourage mild as very sleep:
> Not the hills and waters, fields and wildwood bowers,
> Smile or speak more tenderly, clothed with peace more deep,
> Here than memory whispers of days our memories keep
> Fast with love and laughter and dreams of withered hours.
> Bright were these with blossoms of old, and though endears
> Still the fair soft phantoms that pass with smiles or tears,

Sweet as roseleaves hoarded and dried wherein we trace
Still the soul and spirit of sense that lives and cheers,
Dawn and noon and sunset are one before they face,"

"City lulled asleep by the chime of passing years;
Sweeter smiles they rest than the radiance round thy peers;
Only love and lovely remembrance here have place.
Time on thee lies lighter than music on men's ears;
Dawn and noon and sunset are one before they face."

Epilogue

IN OCTOBER 1938 A BRILLIANT SOCIAL GATHERING TOOK place at Bath. Marina, Duchess of Kent, danced at the re-opening of the Assembly Rooms in the presence of a gay throng of delighted people. It was a perfect period piece. The fashions and the dances of the eighteenth century were sedulously rehearsed by the assembled company. All was gaiety and mirth.

Less than four years after, in April 1942, German bombers visited the city on one of their "Baedeker" raids and the Assembly Rooms are now a hollow shell. "It was on the evening of Saturday, April 25th, that the sirens sounded. . . . A savage attack that started before midnight and was broken by a short lull was followed after a few hours' pause by a second attack which lasted until just before daybreak on Sunday; and these were succeeded an hour or so after midnight on Sunday by a raid, which, though it lasted only two hours, was even more deadly. Incendiaries and high explosive bombs of all calibres rained on the city. Planes roared down in dive-bombing attacks to as low as 50 feet, and then mercilessly fired on streets and buildings with cannon and machine-gun." Had not Goering boasted, "When I hear the word culture, I reach for my gun"?

In spite of the destruction of the Assembly Rooms, of which little now remains save the outer walls, and the damage caused to a number of the modern churches and hospitals, one is amazed at the smallness of the irreparable injury that the Luftwaffe has been able to inflict on the Queen City of the West. Two houses in the Royal Crescent were gutted by fire but their outer fabric still stands in all its majestic loveliness. Similarly, the Circus, though damaged by fire at the corner where Bennett Street leads to the Assembly Rooms, still retains intact its tremendous façade of Doric, Ionic, and Corinthian columns. Lansdown Place East and Lansdown Place West—the two wings to Lansdown Crescent—were very badly damaged, but the Crescent itself has escaped the worst of the onslaught. There is a hideous gap in the south side of Queen Square, which is as much

82   April, 1942: Lansdown Place East, after the Blitz

83, 84 Bath Chairs

to be deplored as the destruction of the Upper Rooms. Avon Street and the poor quarters near the river and the station bore the brunt of the devastation.

Bath bears her scars bravely. Her head is proud and erect, for in her two thousand years of recorded history she has seen much of pagan hatred and fury. In historical perspective the latest Teutonic assault cannot seem much more formidable than the onslaught of Angles and Saxons on the peaceful undefended Aquae Sulis. Conscious of the greatness of her historic past, Bath can afford to endure the present and to contemplate the future with a lustrous calm born of ripe experience.

Bibliography

Besides such contemporary accounts of Bath as those contained
in the writings of John Leland, Celia Fiennes, Oliver Goldsmith,
Tobias Smollett, Jane Austen, and many others mentioned in the
foregoing pages, these works have been of great assistance to me:

AUSTEN-LEIGH, EMMA. *Jane Austen and Bath.* (1939).

BARBEAU, M. *Life and Letters at Bath in the Eighteenth Century.*
(1902).

BRAKSPEAR, SIR HAROLD. *Bath Abbey.* (1940 ed.).

BRITTON, JOHN. *History and Antiquities of Bath Abbey.* (1825).

CASSAN, S. H. *Lives of the Bishops of Bath and Wells.* (1829).

EARLE, JOHN. *Bath Ancient and Modern.* (1864).

EGAN, P. *Walks Through Bath.* (1819).

GREEN, MOWBRAY A. *The Eighteenth Century Architecture of Bath.*
(1904).

HAVERFIELD, F. J. "Romano-British Somerset" in *Victoria County
History of Somerset.* Vol. I (1906).

HESSELGRAVE, R. A. *Lady Miller and the Batheaston Literary Circle.*
(1927).

HOLMES, CHANCELLOR T. S. "Bath Cathedral Priory" in *Victoria
County History of Somerset.* Vol. II (1911).

HUNT, W. (Editor). *Two Chartularies of Bath Priory.* (Somerset
Record Society, 1893).

KING, A. J., and WATTS, B. H. (Editors). *Municipal Records of
Bath 1189 to 1604* (n.d.).

MELVILLE, LEWIS. *Bath under Beau Nash—and after.* (1926 ed.)

SCARTH, H. M. *Aquae Sulis.* (1864).

SITWELL, EDITH. *Bath.* (1932).

SMITH, R. A. L. "John of Tours, Bishop of Bath, 1088–1122"
in *Downside Review.* XX (1942).

WARD, LOCK, AND CO. *Bath.* (n.d.).

WARDLE, F. D. (Editor). *Bath Chamberlains' Accounts, 1568–1602.*
(Somerset Record Society, 1923).

WARNER, R. *History of Bath.* (1801).

Index

The Numerals in italic type denote the figure numbers of illustrations.

115

INDEX

INDEX

INDEX